P9-AOY-409

1990
GREEN
COIN
BOOK

1990 GREEN COIN BOOK

Nineteenth Edition

A complete, illustrated catalog of U.S. coins
and bills and their cash premium values
from 1652 to the present
and
The complete coinage of Canada and Newfoundland
from 1858 to date

BY ROBERT FRIEDBERG
EDITED BY ARTHUR L. AND IRA S. FRIEDBERG

Associate Editor: Arthur S. Goldenberg

Bell Publishing Company
New York

This 1990 edition is published by Bell Publishing Company, distributed by Crown Publishers, Inc., 225 Park Avenue South, New York, New York 10003, by arrangement with Mr. Arthur L. Friedberg and Mr. Ira S. Friedberg.

Originally published as *The Green Coin Book Appraising and Selling Your Coins*

Printed and Bound in the United States of America

ISBN 0-517-69093-4
h g f e d c b a

CONTENTS

A Note from the Publishers

The cash premium values in this book are published for the information and guidance of all concerned — for those who have coins for sale as well as for those who want a complete reference work on the market value of coins and currency.

The valuations listed do not indicate retail prices, but instead, closely approximate how much established coin dealers will actually pay for any material needed in their stock. The valuations are based on the coins being in Good to Very Good condition, unless otherwise noted. Coins in better condition are worth more.

The editors are professional coin dealers. Anyone interested in either buying or selling coins and paper money may contact them at the following address: The Coin & Currency Institute, Inc., P.O. Box 1057, Clifton, NJ 07014. When shipping coins, be sure to use insured or registered mail.

Since silver and gold have risen to their current levels, the values of many coins are based on their precious metal content. Most coin dealers are paying a premium over face value for any and all of these silver coins regardless of date or condition; in many cases, even uncirculated coins are not worth more than their melt value. For the purpose of this book, silver has been calculated at $7.50 per ounce, and gold at $425.00 per ounce. Therefore, all dimes, quarters and half dollars which are valued at $.45, $1.15 and $2.25 respectively, and many United States gold coins, fluctuate in relation to the commodity price of silver and gold and their actual premium value will vary accordingly.

Because of this, the cash premium values of Silver coins, dollars, Commemorative Half Dollars, Proof & Mint sets and gold coins are subject to fluctuation.

Do not clean or polish any coins! They will lose a great deal of their premium value if you do. Coins should be left in the same condition as when found, no matter how dark they may appear.

The American Eagles

These coins were approved by Congress and first released by the mint in the fall of 1986. Although each coin bears a denomination, the uncirculated versions are bought and sold strictly on the basis of their gold or silver content and bullion prices at the time of the transaction. The proof versions were intended for collectors and were sold by the mint at a premium over bullion content.

Type: Silver Eagle

Denom	*Date*	**Unc**	**Proof**
1 Dollar	1986	**10.00**	**20.00**
1 Dollar	1987	**6.00**	**17.00**
1 Dollar	1988	**6.00**	**17.00**

Type: Gold Eagle

Denom	Date	Unc	Proof
5 Dollars (1/10 oz)	1986	**35.00**	**none**
	1987	**35.00**	**none**
	1988	**35.00**	**55.00**
10 Dollars (¼ oz)	1986	**100.00**	**none**
	1987	**100.00**	**none**
	1988	**100.00**	**110.00**
25 Dollars (½ oz)	1986	**200.00**	**none**
	1987	**200.00**	**275.00**
	1988	**200.00**	**225.00**
50 Dollars (1 oz)	1986	**415.00**	**470.00**
	1987	**415.00**	**500.00**
	1988	**415.00**	**500.00**

Preface

At some time or another almost all of us acquire or come across some coins or old pieces of paper money which excite our curiosity or otherwise hold our interest. What is it about these coins that has thus captured our attention? It may have been the strangeness of denomination (a copper 2 Cent piece or a nickel 3 Cent piece or a silver Half Dime or a 3 Dollar gold piece); it may have been antiquity (a large Cent of 1794 or a Colonial Copper of 1694); or the surprise of discovering for yourself an untoward bit of information (that we once used a 15 Cent piece of paper money that was, and still is, legal tender); it may have been sheer, compelling intrinsic value (any gold coin) or immediate negotiable value (an old large size 5 Dollar bill); or it may have been the historical associations evoked by the coins (the Battle of Gettysburg, the exploits of Daniel Boone, the Landing of the Pilgrims, the discovery of America itself); or perhaps it was the glittering beauty of perfection (a set of current coins in brilliant proof condition, or a single older coin so finely preserved that it assumed the status of a gem in your mind).

No matter which quality it has been, or what circumstance introduced you to the coins, you have held them in your hand, you have scrutinized them (perhaps under a magnifying glass), you have conjured with them in your imagination, and after the first flush of recognition has passed and the pride of ownership has asserted itself, one question, one unknown factor still remains unanswered for you—how much are these coins worth? It is at this point that for you

THE SEARCH FOR RARE COINS

has begun, a pursuit, or pastime, if you will, indulged in passionately by millions of us for pleasure or for profit. That your coins are worth more than their face value, there is somehow no doubt in your mind. You have been conditioned to believe it, or at the least, to hope it, by the larger and larger amounts of rare coin publicity in recent years.

A boy, rummaging around among his grandmother's effects, finds an 1856 Flying Eagle Cent and sells it to a coin dealer for several hundred dollars; the story is picked up by a news association and is carried in the daily press from coast to coast—or the Treasury Department throws into circulation through the banking system several million silver dollars (as it did in the mid-1960's)—coins which had lain in the vaults for a generation, undisturbed, still in bright, newly minted condition and containing many dates considered rare. The story is headlined in a great eastern daily and almost at once the switchboard of a leading coin dealer is clogged with thousands of incoming phone calls—urgent inquiries from both buyers and sellers—or a banker leaves a map with his will, leading to a hoard of gold coins buried on his estate. The government seizes the coins, you read about it, you hear about it, and you wait to see if the heirs will ever get the coins. The story has a happy ending; they do. The government says that all gold coins may be freely bought and sold or otherwise traded in.

On the other hand, you may have heard some tales about coins that are not quite authentic. You cannot find a 1913 Liberty Head Nickel, because only five pieces were minted and all are accounted for in known collections; and the likelihood of finding an 1804 Silver Dollar or a 5 Dollar gold piece of 1822, or a Brasher Doubloon challenges the laws of probability; no U.S. coin has ever been called in because of a defect in the design; the Columbian Half Dollar of 1892 is *not* worth $10,000.00, as was once mistakenly reported.

The so-called fabulous coins do, of course, exist, but they are not easily to be found or had. The great rarities of U.S. coinage—the pieces that bring many hundreds of dollars—were recognized as rare and valuable almost immediately after striking and they have been jealously guarded ever since by the intelligent, well-informed and alert collectors in each generation. Therefore, if one does come across an 1827 Quarter, or an 1838-O Half-Dollar, or an 1804 Silver Dollar; if you should have a 3 Dollar gold piece of 1875 or a 4 Dollar gold piece of 1880 or a 5 Dollar gold piece of 1815, then it is most likely that these coins were originally purchased as rare collectors items for large sums of money, and have come from a highly regarded coin collection, rather than from the accumulated small change of bygone days.

But instead of a few dozen legendary pieces, we still have the main output of U.S. coinage for our field of activity, containing, as it does, multitudes of coins with cash premium values ranging from the modest to the substantial. It is the search for, and the recognition of these coins that is occupying so many millions of Americans today, for pleasure as a pastime or for business as a profession. It is for them and for you that this volume has been created, and in our attempt to make it the finest and most useful coin book of its kind in existence it has of necessity become

A COMPLETE CATALOGUE OF U.S. COINS

from 1652 to date, including the pre-revolutionary Colonial coinage as well as the Pioneer gold coinage struck after the California gold rush at the various Territorial Mints.

We have thus accounted for all the "hard money" that has ever been issued in this country; but what of our paper money? The first U.S. Government notes were issued in 1861 and since then many rare and valuable notes have been produced, including some of quite recent years. These are just as much sought after and collected as are coins and for many years now currency for collectors has assumed an importance equal to that of coins.

We have therefore decided to present the subject of American monetary issues in its entirety and accordingly you will find in this book, as an adjunct to the coin listing, a companion catalogue of

ALL TYPES AND SERIES OF U.S. PAPER MONEY

ALL TYPES OF CONFEDERATE PAPER MONEY

from 1861 to the present day and including (a) the early large size notes, (b) the later or present size notes, (c) Fractional Currency issues—the 3, 5, 10, 15, 25 and 50 Cent notes which circulated as U.S. paper money in the 1860's and 1870's, and which are still legal tender, (d) Confederate Money from the 50 Cent note to the 1000 Dollar note.

The tabular arrangement used in cataloguing the paper money has been designed for efficient use and the information given is both concise and complete, so that even without illustrations, you will be able to locate and identify any note without any confusion.

The concluding section of this book is devoted to the coinage of our neighbors to the north, with whom we share such a long common border. As with the U.S. coinage, we have aimed for thorough coverage and in these pages you will also find a complete catalogue of

THE COINS OF CANADA AND NEWFOUNDLAND

together with those of New Brunswick, Nova Scotia, Prince Edward Island and British Columbia. The Canadian series begins in 1858 when the first, true coins on the Dollar or Decimal standard were issued.

The inclusion of the Canadian series in this catalogue is not an afterthought but is rather dictated by the existing necessity for this information, since the Canadian issues rank next in popularity to U.S. coins. Canadian coins are now considered as important as our domestic coins, and in some sections of the country they form the major part of numismatic activity. A glance at the catalogue will reveal many coins with high premium values and an active interest in the coinage of British North America can prove to be a rewarding experience.

With the inclusion of the Canadian series in this volume the publishers believe this to be

A UNIQUE BOOK

in the annals of numismatic literature, since never before has so much varied and useful information been offered in a single, low-priced, convenient book. For example, until now there has never been a listing in the same book of the premium values of paper money together with coins. The premium books of the past have rarely had listings with any completeness of both Colonial coins and Pioneer gold coins.

It is thus believed that by the proper reference to this book, one should be able to evaluate any coin of American origin, any type of U.S. or Confederate paper money and any coin in the British North American series.

It is important at this point to attempt an answer to the question

WHAT MAKES A COIN VALUABLE?

a perplexing and sometimes vexing question. At the outset let it be said that mere age alone has nothing to do with establishing the value of a coin. Many persons mistakenly regard the figure 100 with especial reverence, thinking that the age of 100 years or more automatically confers a special value on a coin. This is simply not so, as an analysis of the coin valuations will reveal. For example, the 1794 Cent commands a premium of $50.00, but the 1914-D Cent brings $32.00. A bronze coin of ancient Greece from about 350 B.C. can be bought for about $20.00; a silver coin of Rome from about 200 A.D. for about $40.00; an English Shilling of Queen Elizabeth dated 1587 for about $15.00—and so on—yet a *1932-D Quarter—only 57 years old at the present writing has a premium value of $20.00.*

There are actually three factors which combine to determine the cash premium value of any coin, namely, rarity, demand and condition. The first of these

RARITY

is the most important, since without rarity, the other two factors are only of minor significance. A coin becomes rare out of various circumstances; it may be struck in much fewer numbers than is normal for a contemporary coin of that type (witness the 1877 Cent, the 1931-S Cent, the 1885 Nickel, the 1916-D Dime, the 1901-S Quarter); or it may be a coin of a type struck in only one year (witness the 1793 Half-Cent, the 1796 Quarter, the 1808 Quarter Eagle, the 1907 Double Eagle with Roman numerals); or it may be a coin struck in relatively large numbers for the period but of which only a very few have survived (witness the 1802 Half-Dime, the 1873-CC Dime, the 1876-CC 20 Cent piece, the 1822 Half-Eagle); or it may be one of the fabled pieces of which so few were struck to begin with that it became a great rarity on the day of minting (witness the 1913 Liberty Head Nickel, the 1894-S Dime, the 1804 Silver dollar, the 1885 Trade dollar, any proof coin before 1858); or, as is also likely, the rarity may be determined by the condition of the coin. In these days when millions of collectors are competing for and buying up the choicest specimens, coins which may be very common in used or circulated condition have become quite rare in new or uncirculated condition (witness the entire series of 10, 25 and 50 cent pieces from 1892 to 1933, all Liberty Head nickels, most Indian Head cents, early Lincoln cents with mint marks, etc.). In fact almost any uncirculated coin before about 1930 is now considered scarce in one degree or another.

Assuming then that a given coin is of some rarity, another factor that determines its value is

DEMAND

which is both judge and jury and your only true indicator of the coin's popularity in the numismatic market place. No matter how rare a coin may be, it cannot be easily sold for a price commensurate with its rarity, unless there is a demand for it by collectors. This demand manifests itself to the professional coin dealer through his customers. Repeated requests for a coin not in his stock automatically create a demand for that coin, and if he wishes to stay in business, he must sooner or later buy it. The ultimate demand is thus created by the ultimate consumer, the collector himself, but the large amounts of cash that support the numismatic market are furnished by the professional coin dealers, who thus perform an essential service for both seller and buyer.

It is obvious that all coins cannot be equally in demand at all times; that is why so many coins appear to have a value disproportionately high or low in relation to their rarity. As mentioned above, demand, and hence value, is created by the mass of collectors who are subject to all sorts of collecting impulses. Hence there are fashions, changes of taste and recurrent cycles in coin collecting, as there are in other cultural pursuits. One year Roosevelt Dimes may be the rage; the next year Franklin Half-Dollars; then it may be Proof Sets or Commemoratives or rolls of coins.

But out of all the welter of intense numismatic activity, one trend remains constant through the years—the lower the denomination of the coin, the greater the demand. Hence the King of American coins is the Cent. There are millions more who collect cents—Lincoln and Indian—than any other coins; many more who collect dimes than quarters; many more who collect silver dollars than 5 dollar gold pieces; and many more who collect 20 dollar gold pieces than 50 Dollar bills.

One example selected out of many will show how demand is uncompromising and inexorable in determining coin values. The 1914-D Lincoln cent with a coinage of 1,193,000 pieces has a listed premium value of $32.00, but the 1914-S Quarter with a much smaller coinage of 264,000 pieces lists at only $6.50; compare both with the Cent of 1814—a hundred years earlier—which has a coinage of 357,800 pieces and a listed value of $13.00. Obviously, the 1914-D Cent will tend to keep increasing in value, whereas the other two coins will tend to remain about as they are—unless there is a radical change in collecting habits.

An analysis of the material in this book will reveal much interesting and some surprising data about our coins and their values. Fortunately for numismatics, there are now so many collectors clamoring for all types of coins and there is so much nationwide interest in coin and currency collecting, that one will find a ready sale for almost any American coin, providing always, of course, that it is in suitable

CONDITION

for collecting purposes, since condition, or the state of preservation, is the third factor that helps determine the value of a coin.

Regarded purely as objects of the past (a Greek urn, a Flemish tapestry, a Colt firearm), coins are desired by collectors in the finest condition in which they can be found, within a given price range. Some can afford the finest pieces, others only the average ones. Perhaps this love of new, beautiful coins goes back to our childhood. How pleased we were to be given a new, shiny coin in our change and how reluctant we were to spend it! The true collector among us did not spend it but put it away—if he could afford it—and when found again many years later, it would still be in new condition and by then it would have gained something else—numismatic value.

In this respect a new coin can be likened to a beautiful woman in the full bloom of her youth—lustrous, desirable and admired by all; but as she circulates through the days and years of her life, subtle changes occur in her appearance and after a certain length of time she bears little resemblance to the thing she once was; only her identity is the same; but if only she were the Sleeping Beauty of the fable, she would be found one hundred years later, still lustrous, desirable and admired by all. Coins have become the true sleeping beauties of our generation and there are many such waiting to be restored to life by the diligent prince charmings who will discover them in their "piggy" banks, attics, family souvenirs, bank vaults, or among long-forgotten, unused possessions.

The condition of a very rare coin is not so important a factor in value as it is of a more common coin. The rare piece would be valuable in its own right and the difference in value between the best and poorest condition would not be too great. Some series of coins tend to exist in choice condition, others in poor condition. For example, most modern silver coins exist in well preserved, brilliant condition and there is not much difference in value between an average used piece and a new one. (From about 75 cents to $1.25 for a common silver Washington Quarter.) Early Large Cents, on the other hand, exist mostly in quite worn condition and new pieces are very rare indeed (from about $55.00 to $1,000.00 for the Large Cent of 1795). Among other recent coins for example the 1927-S

Quarter in average used condition has a premium listing of only $4.00 but a new or uncirculated specimen can easily be sold for $1500.00 because it is so very rare in this choice condition. Similarly, from used to new, the 1926-S Nickel ranges from $2.75 to about $400.00, the 1921 Half-Dollar from $22.50 to about $2,000.00; the 1927-D Dime from $1.00 to about $250.00. But the 1909-S-VDB Cent, which is a rare coin in any condition, has a narrow range of values, and a used piece brings about $150.00, a new piece about $300.00.

It is thus evident that condition is intimately tied to rarity and hence to demand, and it is these three factors operating together in various proportions that determine the price at which a coin can be sold at a given time in a given place.

The condition of a coin is usually denoted by a degree of fineness. (Please note that the numismatic meaning of the word "fine" is quite different from its literary meaning, as will be seen below.) The standard terms used in grading the condition of coins, their abbreviations, and what the terms mean are as follows:—

PROOF or PR. The ultimate condition of coins, since proof coins are struck purely for collectors and not for circulation. The greatest care is lavished in their production so that they will emerge as supreme examples of the art of coinage. A premium over face value has always been charged by the Mint for its proof coins. The coins are struck from scientifically polished dies and metal blanks, and the resultant proof coins are easily recognized by their unusual brilliance. They shine like no other coins you have ever seen, because the surface of a proof coin is like that of a spotless mirror. You can actually see yourself in one of these coins.

UNCIRCULATED or UNC. This denotes a coin in new or unused condition and Unc. coins are usually in the same brilliant condition as when they left the mint. That shiny coin you sometimes get from your bank is considered an Unc. coin if you are the first person to whom this coin has been paid out in the normal course of coin distribution from government mint to local bank via the Federal Reserve System. As soon as you have put your finger marks on the coin and let it jingle in your pocket with other coins for any length of time, it is no longer considered Unc. in the true sense of the word.

EXTREMELY FINE or EF. This denotes a coin which has been in circulation so little, that it shows only the slightest sign of wear or use. For the most part, an EF coin still retains the lustre or mint bloom of an

Unc. piece. Actually many EF coins are truly Unc. pieces which have been poorly handled through the years, so that they now show slight friction, minor abrasions or other unimportant blemishes.

VERY FINE or VF. A coin described as VF will generally have been in circulation a relatively short time. It will certainly show evidence of use such as loss of lustre, wear on the highest struck portions, and a proportionate amount of small surface markings which, however, do not detract from the over-all choiceness of true VF quality. Every detail of lettering and design that was originally impressed into the coin will be boldly visible. In general, a coin taken out of your change at random, that is from one to two years old, will tend to be in VF condition.

FINE or F. A fine coin has begun to show signs of more obvious circulation and can best be recognized by the letters and numerals appearing on it. By now they have become somewhat thick and blurry from the constant soft friction of circulation. All of the larger letters will be fully visible but the smaller ones may have begun to fade in a coin rated as fine. If the coin is silver, the reeding or milling on the edge will have begun to lose its character, and is approaching the point when it will vanish from the coin altogether, leaving it with a smooth edge. A truly fine coin makes an overall pleasing impression on the eye, as the amount of circulation is nicely and evenly distributed over its entire surface, but is still not severe enough to give the coin a shopworn appearance.

VERY GOOD and GOOD or VG and G. These two terms are all-embracing in scope because they accurately describe the condition of most of the millions of non-current coins now in existence. (By non-current we mean all types of coins except those presently being struck.) These terms are used singly as VG and G or sometimes together as G-VG. Coins in either of these two conditions (between which there is only a minor difference in value) are the general, run-of-the-mill, circulated coins found everywhere. They have spent long, faithful years in the service of ther country and they look it. The reason so very many of our older type coins are found in this condition is that there were few coin collectors in the old days. Consequently most coins got into circulation and stayed there for many years, passing routinely into the government melting pot or casually into a private holding.

G and VG coins present a well-worn appearance and are in a more advanced state of circulation than fine coins. Most of the larger letters will have shrunk somewhat from the creeping paralysis of circulation, moving from the outer edge of the coin to the center. The smaller lettering may have disappeared altogether, such as the word "Liberty" which appears on the head band of a Liberty-head coin or on an Indian Head Cent. But such coins are still recognizable for what they are; you can easily read the date, the denomination, the main legends and the mint mark, if any. Just as they are the most common, so are they the most widely collected, because they represent decent, collectible coins at moderate prices, the appeal thus being to the great mass of collectors.

In this book, for example, the valuations are based on the coins being in G-VG condition, except as noted elsewhere in the catalogue proper.

FAIR and POOR. These two terms (no standard abbreviations) are used for coins in the lowest possible condition. Such coins are so badly worn or have such defects, that they are barely recognizable and hence are called "space fillers." They will do in a collection simply because better ones cannot be found or may cost too much. Only very rare coins would command a premium in fair or good condition. Such coins might be a 1793 Half-Cent or Cent, a 1794 Dollar, or 1796 Half-cent, Quarter, or Half-Dollar, etc. Fair and poor coins present an appearance which some have described as miserable. Most of the design and lettering are gone and so little remains on the coin that sometimes only experienced numismatic deduction can properly attribute it.

Sometimes coins will be found that cannot properly be described by any of the above conditions because they have been mutilated in various ways or are false. **Such coins are of no numismatic value and command no premium.** If genuine, they are worth only their face amount, but if a hole has been drilled into any coin it has lost even its face value, since the government will not redeem such a coin. Some of these various mutilations, defects or deceptions are described as follows:—

HOLED. A coin with a hole drilled completely through it.

PLUGGED HOLE. A holed coin in which the hole has been filled in with some metal to reduce the ugliness of the coin.

LOOPED. A coin with a loop attached to the edge by solder, enabling it to be attached to a chain. This is most common in gold coins.

LOOP REMOVED. A coin from which a loop has been removed by breaking or sawing it off. The edge of the coin will usually reveal evidence of a former loop.

GILDED. Any coin which has been gold plated.

NAMES and INITIALS. These will sometimes be found scratched, engraved or stamped on coins. Only in the case of a great rarity would a coin thus mutilated command a premium.

ELECTROTYPE. A false coin made by making impressions of a genuine coin on a thin shell of the same metal. The Obv. and Rev. are on different shells, which are then joined after filling them with a cheap alloy to give them weight. A thin line running around the edge will usually identify an electrotype, as well as the fact that it will not have the true ring of a genuine coin.

CAST. A false coin made by making a cast from a genuine coin. Casts can generally be identified by a rough, mottled surface.

ALTERED DATE. A false coin made by changing the date on a genuine coin to another date of much greater rarity and value. Some altered date coins are very difficult to detect and hence dangerous, bearing in mind that the coin itself is genuine. A strong magnifier will generally discover this deception.

MINT MARK ADDED OR REMOVED. Similar in principle to altered date coins, but in this case, the mint mark, not the date, has been tampered with. A mint mark may be added to a coin or removed from it, in order to make it more valuable. As with altered date coins, a strong magnifier should be used on a suspected piece.

POLISHED COINS. Although not mutilated, coins which have been polished to a high shine by cleaning powders, polishing creams, or other abrasives lose a great deal of their premium value, even if in otherwise choice condition. Coins should be left in the same state of preservation as when found, and no attempt should be made to clean or polish them, no matter how dirty they may appear.

TOKENS—CALIFORNIA GOLD PIECES

Sometimes copper or nickel pieces will be found which appear to be U.S. coins and yet cannot be located in this book, which is complete insofar as U.S. coinage is concerned. Such pieces will no doubt turn out to be privately struck tokens of the 19th century. Enormous amounts of these were made during the late 1830's and early 1860's. In both cases the tokens were issued to relieve shortages of small change and they actually circulated as 1 Cent pieces; the early pieces being the size of large Cents and called "Hard Times Tokens"; the later pieces being the size of small Cents and called "Civil War Cents." Such tokens generally have a cash premium value of from $1.00 to $2.00 each.

Other coins which appear to be U.S. pieces are the so-called California gold coins. Like the tokens described above, they are not really coins but private issues; in neither case were they struck under authority of the U.S. Government, nor did they emanate from any government mint.

These California gold pieces—also called charms—exist in denominations of ¼, ½ and 1 Dollar; they may be round or they may be octagonal in shape; they are quite tiny and very thin and they may, or may not, be of gold; some of them have been restruck in recent years.

They were first made in the middle of the 19th Century, ostensibly to augment the gold coins then in circulation out west. It is doubtful if they ever served that purpose, because their minute size and insubstantial weight must have made them impossible to handle with any assurance of safety.

Those pieces are considered to be the original issues which are struck in genuine gold and have the word, "Dollar" or "Dol" as part of the denomination. In this case they have a value ranging from about $25.00 to $50.00 Any other pieces are worth considerably less.

APPRAISING AND SELLING YOUR COINS

If you have any U.S. coins or currency for sale or any Canadian coins, it would be prudent to acquaint yourself with the contents of this book, so that you can be better informed and be guided accordingly.

This book has been so prepared that by proper reference to the catalogue section as well as to this Preface and to the General Information which follows, you will be able to appraise your coins yourself and estimate their cash value with a fair degree of accuracy. The following points should be borne in mind when appraising and selling your coins:—

PRICE. **The cash premium values in this book reflect the approximate prices that established, professional coin dealers will pay for material. These values, which are averages, have been arrived at by a careful study of many years duration of market conditions and buying trends from coast to coast. Since the valuations are averages, the price actually offered may vary from the published values.**

SUPPLY. Sometimes a dealer will not wish to buy certain coins—even high-premium pieces—because he has an ample supply of them at the time of offer. In this respect he is like any other merchant who has to exercise a certain amount of inventory control to keep him from getting unhealthily overstocked in any one item.

DEMAND. On the other hand, if your coins are popular issues and continually in demand, the dealer will be tempted to buy them even though he has an ample stock. In this case, he is taking a calculated risk, based on his experiences and judgment, and he is gambling either that the demand will continue strong or that the coins will enhance in value.

RARITY. In general, the higher the premium value of the coin, the easier it will be to sell. A coin with a value very much above its face value, or very much above the average for that type, will tend to be a scarce coin in short supply and hence in demand.

CONDITION. The values in this book are based on the condition in which the coins are most frequently found, namely, good to very good, as has been proven by experience. If your coins are in much choicer condition they will command a higher price than listed; if in inferior condition either a lower price, or no premium at all, will prevail. In some cases, as will be noted in the catalogue, the valuations are for uncirculated or proof specimens. In the case of all gold coins the valuations are for specimens in choice, well preserved condition, ranging from extremely fine to uncirculated.

CLEANING. As noted earlier, coins should be left in the same condition as when found. No attmept should be made to alter their appearance by cleaning or polishing.

COIN DEALERS. Coins and currency should be offered to professional coin dealers established in a regular place of business. For a list of the coin dealers in any community, consult the local classified telephone directory under the heading "Coin Dealers," or those Sunday newspapers that have a Stamp and Coin section and carry the advertising of coin dealers. The material you have may be brought to them in person or it may be shipped in for their inspection and offer, or a list of it may be sent by mail to see if they are interested.

MINT AND MINT MARKS—ABBREVIATIONS

The capital letters you will see after certain dates represent mint marks. They appear in this manner: 1853-O, 1878-S, 1890-CC, etc. The actual spot on the coin where the mint mark may be found is indicated clearly in the catalogue, before the listing of each type of coin. The letters and the mints they represent are as follows (please remember that coins struck at the Philadelphia mint do not have a mint mark except as noted below):—

C—Charlotte, N.C. On gold coins only from 1838-1861.
CC—Carson City, Nev. On gold and silver coins from 1870-1893.
D—Dahlonega, Ga. On gold coins only from 1838-1861.
D—Denver, Colo. On all coins from 1906-1964, 1968 to date.
O—New Orleans, La. On gold and silver coins from 1838-1909.
P—Philadelphia, Pa. On nickels from 1942-1945. On Anthony dollars from 1979 to date. On nickels, dimes, quarters and half dollars from 1980 to date.
S—San Francisco, Calif. On all coins from 1854-1955, 1968 to date.
W—West Point, N.Y. On the $10.00 1984 Olympic commemoratives, and the $5.00 1986 Statue of Liberty commemorative.

CANADIAN ISSUES

H—Heaton Mint in Birmingham, England.
C—Ottawa Mint in Canada.
No mint mark—Before 1908, London and after 1908, Ottawa.

Abbreviations for the condition of coins are given under the heading "Condition" (see above). Other abbreviations used are:

OBV.—Obverse or the "head" side of a coin.
REV.—Reverse or the "tail" side of a coin.
ARR.—Arrows, as on certain silver coins from 1853-1855 and 1873-1874.

In the General Information, which follows, you will find important data on various coins.

GENERAL INFORMATION

(Notes and comments on various coins, giving more specific or detailed information than is to be found in the catalogue proper.)

COLONIAL AND STATE COINAGE

Many of these coins are so rare, that forgeries have been created. There are various types of these forgeries, such as electrotypes, casts and struck copies. The last type is especially difficult to recognize since the forged piece is struck from an actual die manufactured for that purpose. In general, any very rare Colonial coin in really first class condition should be suspected of being a forgery or other type of facsimile, and all such pieces should be authenticated.

CAROLINA ELEPHANT TOKEN COINAGE. A very rare variety has the spelling "Proprieters." Forgeries exist.

CONNECTICUT. Higley Token Coinage. Forgeries exist. There is also a unique variety in which a wheel appears on the Rev. In the State Coinage, there are very many minor varieties in the appearance of the bust and in the spelling of the legends.

MARYLAND. Forgeries exist of the Lord Baltimore Penny, which is a very rare coin. The head on the 3 Pence piece of Standish Barry is reputed to be that of Washington. This coin has the date as "July 4, 90."

MASSACHUSETTS. Forgeries exist of the NE coinage and of the Oak Tree and Pine Tree issues. In the State Coinage there is a rare variety of the 1787 Cent in which the eagle holds the bundle of arrows in the right talon, rather than in the left one.

NEW ENGLAND COINAGE. The Elephant Half Penny of 1694 is similar in design to the Carolina Half Penny of 1694. The New England piece, however, is extremely rare and forgeries exist.

NEW HAMPSHIRE. Forgeries are known of the 1776 Cent.

NEW JERSEY. The St. Patrick coins, sometimes attributed to New Jersey, will be found in Part Two, since they bear nothing on them to identify them with New Jersey. A scarce variety of the 1788 Cent shows the horse's head facing to the left.

NEW YORK. Forgeries exist of the Cents of Gov. Clinton, of the "Non VI . . ." type, of the Indian type and of the Excelsior type. A unique specimen is known of a New York Cent which shows the head of George III on one side and a standing Indian on the other. There are several varieties of the 1787 Cent with laureate male bust. These varieties are called "Nova Eboracs" (New Yorks). The bust may differ in size or the seated figure may face either to right or left.

UNITED STATES OF AMERICA. The 1792 coinage of the U.S. Mint has traditionally been catalogued with Colonial Coins, the whole forming the subject of Early American Coins. The 1792 coins were experimental and all are very rare and seldom met with, except for the Half Disme. Regular U.S. coinage began in 1793. (The illustration of the 1792 Cent with silver center does not show the silver center.)

On the other hand, the Fugio Cents of 1787 were the first coins issued under the authority of the United States Government and were reportedly struck at New Haven. These actually circulated and are far commoner than the 1792 issues.

CONFEDERATIO COINAGE. Forgeries exist of the 1785 Cent.

THE CONTINENTAL DOLLAR. On some varieties, the word is spelled as "Curency." Forgeries and imitations are known.

NOVA CONSTELLATIO—IMMUNE COLUMBIA COINAGE. The "U.S." that appears on the Rev. of the 1783-1786 Cents may be either in block letters or in a script monogram. On some varieties the word is spelled as "Constelatio." Forgeries are known of the 1785 Cents inscribed "Immune Columbia."

THE TRIANGLE TOKEN. This piece has sometimes been called a Kentucky Cent, only because "K" appears at the top of the triangle of 15 rosettes, each bearing an initial of one of the 15 states. Otherwise, this coin does not bear the name of a specific colony.

GEORGE WASHINGTON COINS AND TOKENS. Forgeries are known of most valuable pieces including the 1792 Half Dollars.

UNITED STATES COINS

HALF CENTS. Various type forgeries are known of 1793 and 1796 and electrotype forgeries mainly of 1831, 1836, 1852, and 1840-1848 inclusive.

1797. A rare variety has lettering on the edge.

1808. A scarce variety shows the last 8 struck over a 7.

LARGE CENTS. 1793. All three major varieties of this date have been forged, mainly by electrotyping. "America" on the Chain type sometimes appears as "Ameri"; the wreath type has either lettering on the edge or vines and bars, and there is an extremely rare variety with a strawberry sprig under the head rather than a 3-leaf sprig.

1797. A scarce variety has a stemless wreath on the Rev.

1798. A scarce variety has the Rev. typical of 1796 Cents.

1799. This coin has been extensively forged by altering the date of another Large Cent of similar type to read 1799.

1801. A scarce variety has three errors in the design; there is but one stem to the wreath; the fraction appears as 1/000 and "United" as "Ilnited."

1804. This coin too has been forged by altering the date of another coin.

1815. Cents have been struck in every year from 1793 to date except 1815. In order to maintain an unbroken continuity of years, some collectors have altered other cents to read "1815." An 1815 Cent is therefore a fantasy created by self-delusion.

1839. A rare variety shows the 9 struck over a 6.

FLYING EAGLE CENTS. 1856. More forgeries must exist of this date than of any other U.S. coin. Most of these forgeries are altered dates, which are clearly visible under a strong magnifier; 1858 Cents have been used most often for this alteration, the last 8 being converted into a 6.

INDIAN HEAD CENTS. 1864-L. The L appears as a quite small letter at the end of the ribbon as it trails off the feather head dress on the Indian head.

LINCOLN HEAD CENTS. 1909-VDB. The VDB appears as three small letters at the extreme bottom of the Rev. They indicate the initials of the designer, Mr. Victor D. Brenner.

1914-D. This coin has recently been forged by alteration. A "D" has been added to a plain 1914 Cent or a D mint marked coin ending in a 4 has been changed to 1914.

2 CENT PIECES. 1864 Small Motto. This refers to "In God We Trust." The quickest way to distinguish the small letters in the motto from the large ones in the Large Motto type is to look at the letter D in God. In the Small Motto the D is quite rounded; in the large motto it is narrow and oval.

BUFFALO NICKELS. A scarce variety of 1918-D shows the 8 struck over a 7. The 3-legged buffalo of 1937-D shows the buffalo standing on only three legs, the result of a die defect obliterating the fourth leg.

HALF DIMES. 1796. A rare variety shows the 6 struck over the 5 of 1795.

1872-S. The mint mark may be either within or below the wreath.

DIMES. 1811. All coins are struck over 1809.

1823. All coins are struck over 1822.

1824. All coins are struck over 1822.

1873-CC. Only one specimen is known without arrows at the date.

1875. The S and CC mint marks may be either within or below the wreath.

1942/1. A scarce variety exists on which the 2 is struck over the 1 of 1941.

QUARTERS. 1822. A rare variety shows the 25c on the Rev. struck over 50c.

1823. All coins are struck over 1822.

1825. All coins are struck over other dates.

1828. A rare variety shows the 25c struck over 50c.

1842. A rare variety has a small date and exists in proof condition only.

1853/2. All coins are struck over 1852, and are without arrows. This coin has been forged by changing the last 8 of an 1858 into a 3.

1918-S/17. A scarce variety shows the 8 struck over the 7 of a 1917-S.

HALF DOLLARS. 1795. A rare variety shows a stem with three leaves, rather than two, on the upper part of the branch under each wing of the eagle.

1805-1836. Coins of these years are rich in varieties. There are overdates, small and large dates, small and large letters, etc.

1842-O. A rare variety exists with the date much smaller in size.

1846. A rare variety shows the 6 struck over another 6 at right angles to it.

1846-O. A scarce variety shows the date in much taller numerals.

1847. A rare variety shows the 7 struck over the 6 of an 1846.

1853-O without arrows or rays. This great rarity has been forged by altering the last 8 of an 1858-O to a 3.

1917. The mint marks may appear on the Obv. under the motto or on the Rev. to the left of "Half Dollar."

SILVER DOLLARS. 1797. A rare variety has the Rev. legend in smaller letters with a 9 × 7 arrangement of the stars on the Obv.

1895. This rare coin, which exists in proof condition only, has been forged by removing the mint marks on an 1895-O or 1895-S.

UNITED STATES PROOF SETS

The prices of proof sets are subject to some very sudden changes, either upward or downward. This is caused by the private accumulation of large amounts of sets and the resultant speculation therein.

U.S. SILVER COMMEMORATIVE COINS

GRANT 1922★. This coin has been forged by adding a star to an ordinary Grant Half Dollar. All Grant coins with star should be authenticated.

BOONE, 1934-1938. The small 1934 appears on all issues beginning with 1935. It will be found to the right of the standing figure on the Rev.

U.S. GOLD COMMEMORATIVE COINS

LEWIS AND CLARK ISSUE. The Gold Dollars of this issue tended to be used as jewelry. All specimens should be examined for evidence of loop removed or solder remains.

UNITED STATES GOLD COINS

1 DOLLAR. A minor variety appears in the 1849 coinage. The wreath on the Rev. may form a full circle or an open circle.

2½ DOLLARS. 1802. All coins are struck over 1801.

1806. All coins are struck over 1804 or 1805.

1824. All coins are struck over 1821.

1826. All coins are struck over 1825.

1841. This coin has been forged by removing the mint marks from 1841-C or 1841-D coins.

1854-S. This coin has been forged by adding an S mint mark to an 1854 coin of the Philadelphia Mint.

1863. This coin exists in proof condition only, but forgeries have been made by removing the S from 1863-S coins.

3 DOLLARS. 1873 and 1878. These dates should always be looked at under a magnifier. Many persons have accidentally misread these dates because the 3 and the 8 tend to look similar at first glance.

4 DOLLARS. These pieces should always be authenticated as being of gold. Genuine specimens struck from these dies in minor metals as patterns, have sometimes been gold plated as a deception or as an act of self-delusion.

5 DOLLARS. 1795, 1797 and 1798. These three dates each exist in two distinct types; please see the catalogue for proper attribution.

1802. All coins are struck over 1801.

1803. All coins are struck over 1802.

1825. All coins are struck over 1821 or 1824.

1807 and 1834. These two dates each exist in two distinct types.

1854-S. This very rare coin should always be verified as not being an 1854 Philadelphia coin to which an S has later been added.

1887. This coin was struck only in proof condition but forgeries have been made by removing the S mint mark from an 1887-S.

1909-O. This coin should be carefully examined to verify that the mint mark is genuine, or if genuine, that the O is not being mis-read for a D, since these mint marks are usually quite weak.

10 DOLLARS. 1797. This date exists in two distinct types.

1858. Forgeries have been created by removing the mint marks from 1858-O or 1858-S coins.

1907, 1908. These dates exist in more than one distinct type.

20 DOLLARS. 1861 and 1861-S. Each of these two coins exists as a great rarity when the Rev. design is the Paquet type. This type can be identified by the much taller letters in the legend.

1907, 1908. These dates exist in more than one distinct type.

All rare coins of the Philadelphia Mint should be examined for evidence of removed mint marks.

Rare date issues of the period 1908-1932 are subject to sudden price changes, as large amounts tend to be found unexpectedly from time to time.

In recent years, counterfeit coins, struck in gold, have appeared in all denominations, rare as well as common dates.

PIONEER GOLD COINS

The valuations are for coins in average VG-F condition. Really choice pieces are very rare and would command higher prices. If several varieties exist of a given coin, the valuation is for the commonest one.

NORRIS, GRIEG & NORRIS. A 5 Dollar piece has recently been discovered issued at Stockton rather than San Francisco.

TEMPLETON REID. The only known specimen of the 25 Dollar piece of 1849 was stolen in 1858 from the U.S. Mint collection and has never been recovered.

UNITED STATES PAPER MONEY

CONFEDERATE PAPER MONEY

The valuations given for the large size notes and Fractional Currency are for specimens in presentable, used condition (fine to very fine) and not giving a dirty, shopworn appearance. Notes which are torn, thin from use, very badly wrinkled or generally unattractive, would command a smaller premium than listed or none at all, since currency is collected mainly for the beauty and eye appeal inherent in well preserved specimens. Notes which are in new or unused condition would naturally be purchased at higher prices than listed.

Small size or present day notes, on the other hand, are valued in new condition only. Since the notes are recent and more readily available, they are not generally wanted in used condition.

Those who are interested in a fully illustrated book on U.S. paper money are referred to the standard work on this subject, "Paper Money of the United States" by Robert Friedberg. This complete and definitive volume illustrates front and back of every type of paper money ever issued from the 3 Cent note to the 10,000 Dollar note and from the first year of issue in 1861 to the present day. In addition, all varieties of seals and signatures are listed with collectors' valuations. "Paper Money of the United States" is available at almost any coin dealer or you may write for information to the publishers of this book.

There are many varieties of currency, formed by differences in the seals, signatures, series letters, etc., and in all cases, the valuations are for the commoner varieties.

THE COINAGE OF BRITISH NORTH AMERICA

This series begins with the Canadian issues of 1858, which were the first true coins based on the Canadian Dollar consisting of 100 Cents. Prior to 1858, the coinage in use consisted of a miscellaneous variety of copper tokens based on the English Pound. There are hundreds of varieties of these Penny and Half Penny tokens, most of them of only small value (from about .10 to .50) and they are omitted from this book because they are not considered as coins.

Following the introduction of Canadian coins in 1858, the first coins of Newfoundland were issued in 1865, and of Nova Scotia and New Brunswick in 1861. The only issue of Prince Edward Island was a 1 Cent piece in 1871 and of British Columbia a 10 and 20 Dollar gold piece in 1862. These gold coins, however, were not placed in circulation because of opposition from England.

As with the U.S. coins, the valuations for Canadian coins are based on G-VG condition except where otherwise stated.

In 1936 a small dot was placed under the date on some of the 1, 10 and 25 Cent pieces struck in that year. 25 Cent pieces with the dot are somewhat scarce, but the 1 and 10 Cent pieces are very rare.

The maple leaf on part of the 1947 coinage of all denominations may be found as a quite small symbol to the immediate right of the date.

CANADIAN COIN VARIETIES. There are some variations from the normal among certain Canadian coins, making them of greater scarcity and value. The most important varieties follow.

1 Cent 1859. Struck over 1858.

1 Cent 1891. With a smaller date than normal.

1 Cent 1936. With dot below date.

5 Cents 1858. With a larger date than normal.

5 Cents 1900. With round O's in date rather than oval.

5 Cents 1902-H. With a smaller H mint mark than normal.

5 Cents 1921. Not a variety but very rare as a coin because most of the 2½ million struck were melted down rather than issued.

10 Cents 1893. With the top part of the 3 rounded rather than flat.

10 Cents 1913. With larger leaves on the Rev. than normal.

10 Cents 1936. With dot below date.

25 Cents 1936. WIth dot below the wreath under date.

50 Cents 1921. Like the 5 Cents 1921, not a variety but very rare as a coin because most were melted down.

50 Cents 1946. With part of the design extending into the 6.

50 Cents 1947. With maple leaf and a curved 7 pointing to the right, rather than a straight 7 pointing to the left.

1 Dollar 1947. With a pointed 7 rather than a blunt 7 in the date.

Colonial and State Coinage

(1652–1792)

PART ONE

Coins and tokens issued by or for specific colonies or states. These pieces bear either a state name or a device that identifies the state. The valuations below are for coins in used or circulated condition. Bent and holed coins are worthless.

Collectors should be aware that many of the following pieces exist as casts and electrotypes. These are also worthless.

CAROLINA ELEPHANT TOKEN COINAGE

Elephant. Rev. "GOD PRESERVE CAROLINA AND THE LORDS PROPRIETORS 1694," Copper.

Half Penny 1694 .... **550.00**

CONNECTICUT
Higley Token Coinage

Deer standing. Rev. Three axes. Copper.

3 Pence 1737 .... **2,500.00**

Deer standing. Rev. One large axe. Copper.

3 Pence. No date, 1739 .... **3,500.00**

State Coinage

Laureate bust facing right or left. Rev. Female seated. Copper.

1 Cent 1785, 1786, 1787, 1788 .... **20.00**

KENTUCKY

Myddelton Token Coinage

Liberty stretching hand out to two children. Rev. Female seated with shield.

1 Cent 1796. Struck in copper **3,200.00**
1 Cent 1796. Struck in silver **2,500.00**

MARYLAND

Cecil Calvert (Lord Baltimore) Coinage

Head of Lord Baltimore. Rev. Crowned shield and Roman numeral. Silver.

1 Shilling. No date (1658) **650.00**
6 Pence. No date (1658) **500.00**
4 Pence. No date (1658) **600.00**

Head of Lord Baltimore. Rev. Two flags over crown. Copper.

1 Penny (Denarium). No date (1658) .... **Very Rare**

Annapolis Token Coinage of John Chalmers

Clasped hands in wreath. Rev. Two birds and snake within circle. Silver.

1 Shilling 1783 .... **200.00**

Clasped hands. Rev. Circle of rings. Silver. (This coin sold for $24,200 in 1983)

1 Shilling 1783 .... **Very Rare**

Long cross. Rev. Wreath. Silver.

6 Pence 1783 .... **350.00**

Clasped hands. Rev. Plant in wreath. Silver.

3 Pence 1783 .... **275.00**

Baltimore Token Coinage of Standish Barry

Large male head. Rev. Name and value. Silver.

3 Pence 1790 .... **1,250.00**

MASSACHUSETTS

NE (New England) Coinage

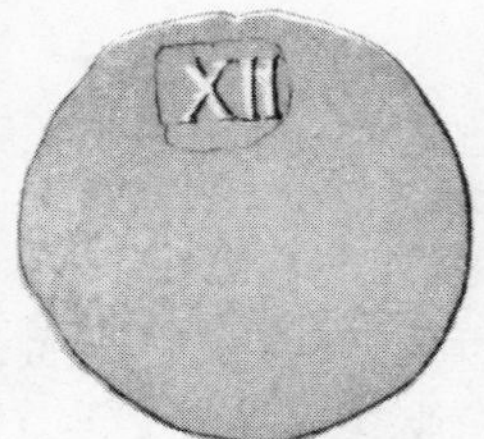

NE at top, the rest blank. Rev. Roman numeral for value at top, the rest blank. Silver.

1 Shilling. No date (1652) **2,500.00**
6 Pence. No date (1652) .... **Very Rare**
3 Pence. No date (1652) .... **Very Rare**

Willow Tree Coinage

A willow tree. Rev. Date and Roman numeral for the value. Silver.

1 Shilling 1652	**1,500.00**
6 Pence 1652	**Very Rare**
3 Pence 1652	**Very Rare**

Oak Tree Coinage

An oak tree. Rev. Date and Roman numeral for the value. Silver.

1 Shilling 1652	**150.00**
6 Pence 1652	**150.00**
3 Pence 1652	**175.00**
2 Pence 1662	**150.00**

Pine Tree Coinage

A pine tree. Rev. Date and Roman numeral for the value. Silver.

1 Shilling 1652. Large size	**175.00**
1 Shilling 1652. Small size	**150.00**
6 Pence 1652	**125.00**
3 Pence 1652	**100.00**

State Coinage

Pine tree. Rev. Female seated on globe. Copper.

1 Cent 1776 . . . . **Unique**

Three heads in Janiform position. Rev. Female seated on globe. Copper.

Half Penny 1776 . . . . **Unique**

Indian standing. Rev. Spread eagle. Copper.

1 Cent 1787, 1788 . . . . **20.00**
Half Cent 1787, 1788 . . . . **22.50**

NEW ENGLAND COINAGE

Elephant Token Coinage

Elephant. Rev. "GOD PRESERVE NEW ENGLAND 1694." Copper.

Half Penny 1694 . . . . **Very Rare**

Lion Token Coinage

Two lions facing in opposite directions. Rev. "NEW ENGLAND." Copper.

Token coin. No date (1675) **700.00**

NEW HAMPSHIRE

Pine tree. Rev. Harp. Copper.

1 Cent 1776 .... **6,000.00**

NEW JERSEY

Horse's head and plow with date below plow. Rev. Shield. Copper.

1 Cent 1786, 1787, 1788 .... **15.00**

Horse's head and plow with date to right of plow. Rev. Shield. Copper.

1 Cent 1786 . . . . **20.00**

Head of Washington. Rev. Spread eagle. Copper.

1 Cent. No date (1786) . . . . —

Head of Washington. Rev. Shield. Copper.

1 Cent. No date (1786) . . . . —

Liberty holding scales, "Immunis Columbia." Rev. Shield. Copper.

1 Cent 1786 . . . . —

Spread eagle. Rev. Shield. Copper.

1 Cent 1786 . . . . —

NEW YORK

State Copper Coinage

Bust of Gov. Clinton. Rev. Shield supported by two figures.

1 Cent 1787 . . . . **2,000.00**

Laureate male bust. Rev. Female seated to right or left.

1 Cent 1787 . . . . **35.00**

Armored bust, "NON VI VIRTUTE VICI." Rev. Liberty holding scales.

1 Cent 1786 . . . . **1,000.00**

Liberty holding scales, "IMMUNIS COLUMBIA." Rev. Eagle.

1 Cent 1787 . . . . **125.00**

Indian standing. Rev. Eagle on globe.

1 Cent 1787 . . . . **2,000.00**

Indian standing. Rev. Shield supported by two figures.

1 Cent 1787 .... **1,500.00**

Shield supported by two figures. Rev. Eagle. The EXCELSIOR cent.

1 Cent 1787 .... **375.00**

Miscellaneous Token Coinage
New Yorke in America Token

Spread eagle. Rev. Two figures under palm tree.

Brass token. No date (1700) **1,500.00**

The Mott Token

Large clock. Rev. Eagle. Copper.

Token 1 Cent 1789 . . . . 35.00

Talbot, Allum & Lee Token

Liberty standing. Rev. Ship. Copper.

1 Cent 1794, 1795 . . . . 20.00

RHODE ISLAND

Admiral Howe's flagship. Rev. Group of ships.

Copper token 1778, 1779 . . . . 250.00

UNITED STATES OF AMERICA

FUGIO CENT COINAGE

Sundial, radiate sun above, and "MIND YOUR BUSINESS" below.
Rev. Circular chain of thirteen links.

1 Cent 1787 . . . . 30.00

EARLY MINT ISSUES

Liberty head. Rev. Flying eagle.

1 Disme 1792. Silver .... **Very Rare**
1 Disme 1792. Copper .... **Very Rare**
Half Disme 1792. Silver **700.00**

Liberty head. Rev. Wreath. With silver center plug.

1 Cent 1792 .... **Very Rare**

Liberty head. Rev. Wreath. The so called Birch Cent, and much larger than the above cent.

1 Cent 1792 .... **Very Rare**

U.S.A. BAR CENT

Monogram of USA. Rev. Thirteen bars. Copper.

1 Cent. No date (1785) **175.00**

VERMONT

Hills over plow. Rev. Radiate eye. Copper.

1 Cent 1785, 1786 .... **45.00**

Male bust. Rev. Seated female, "IMMUNE COLUMBIA." Copper.

1 Cent 1785 .... **850.00**

Male bust to right or left. Rev. Seated female. Copper.

1 Cent 1786, 1787, 1788 .... **45.00**

VIRGINIA

Gloucester Token Coinage

Building. Rev. Star. Brass.

1 Shilling 1714 .... **Very Rare**

English Royal Coinage

Head of George III. Rev. Arms and date.

1 Shilling 1774. Silver .... **Rare**
1 Penny 1773. Copper **3,000.00**
Half penny 1773. Copper **20.00**

Coins and tokens issued for general use in early America and not inscribed with the name of any specific colony or state.

AUCTORI PLEBIS TOKEN COINAGE

Male bust, "AUCTORI PLEBIS." Rev. Seated female. Copper.

1 Cent 1787 .... **20.00**

CONFEDERATIO COINAGE

Figure at pedestal holding bow and arrow. Rev. Thirteen stars in radiate circle. Copper.

1 Cent 1785 .... **Rare**

THE CONTINENTAL DOLLAR

Sundial with radiate sun above. Rev. The names of the thirteen states inscribed on the links of a circular chain. Many copies exist.

1 Dollar 1776. Struck in pewter **500.00**
1 Dollar 1776. Struck in brass .... **Very Rare**
1 Dollar 1776. Struck in silver .... **Very Rare**

GEORGE III—IMMUNE COLUMBIA COINAGE

Head of George III. Rev. Liberty holding scales "IMMUNE COLUMBIA." Copper.

1 Cent 1785 .... **700.00**

GEORGIUS TRIUMPHO TOKEN COINAGE

Laureate male head. Rev. Liberty standing behind screen of thirteen bars. Copper.

1 Cent token 1783 .... **20.00**

NORTH AMERICAN TOKEN

Seated female (Hibernia). Rev. Ship. Copper.

Token coin 1781 . . . . **10.00**

NOVA CONSTELLATIO—IMMUNE COLUMBIA COINAGE

Radiate eye. Rev. "U.S." in wreath. Copper.
(The U.S. in either block or script letters)

1 Cent 1783, 1785, 1786 . . . . **20.00**

Radiate eye. Rev. Liberty holding scales, "IMMUNE COLUMBIA."

1 Cent 1785. Copper . . . . **Rare**
1 Cent 1785. Struck in silver . . . . ——

PITT TOKEN COINAGE

Bust of William Pitt. Rev. Ship and "AMERICA." Copper.

Half penny 1766 .... 60.00
1 Farthing 1766 .... —

PLANTATION TOKEN COINAGE

Horseman and titles of James II of England. Rev. Four shields. Pewter. (This token is sometimes attributed to Florida, but was used in many colonies.)

1/24th Part Real 1688 .... 70.00

ST. PATRICK COINAGE OF MARK NEWBY

(Used Mainly in New Jersey)

St. Patrick standing before throng. Rev. Crowned figure playing harp.

Half Penny. No date (1678). Copper 65.00

St. Patrick holding cross, snakes in foreground. Rev. Crowned figure playing harp.

1 Farthing. No date (1678). Copper 35.00
1 Farthing. Same but struck in silver 450.00

THE TRIANGLE TOKEN

Hand holding scroll. Rev. Triangle formed by fifteen stars, each bearing the initial of a state. K for Kentucky is at top. Copper.

1 Cent. No date (1792) 25.00

VOCE POPULI—HIBERNIA COINAGE

Male bust. Rev. Seated female and "HIBERNIA." Copper.

Half Penny 1760 . . . . 17.50
1 Farthing 1760 . . . . 60.00

WOOD'S COINAGE—HIBERNIA TYPE

Head of George I. Rev. Seated female with harp. Copper.

Half Penny 1722, 1723, 1724 . . . . 15.00
1 Farthing 1722, 1723, 1724 . . . . 15.00

WOOD'S COINAGE—ROSA AMERICANA TYPE

Head of George I. Rev. Rose. Copper.

2 Pence 1722, 1723 or no date **45.00**
1 Penny 1722, 1723 .... **35.00**
Half Penny 1722, 1723 .... **35.00**

GEORGE WASHINGTON COINS AND TOKENS

(All are copper except the Half Dollars of 1792)

Obv: Military bust. "WASHINGTON & INDEPENDENCE."
Rev: Liberty seated. "UNITED STATES."

1 Cent 1783 .... **15.00**

Obv: Head. "WASHINGTON & INDEPENDENCE."
Rev: Liberty seated. "UNITED STATES."

1 Cent 1783 .... 15.00

Obv: Head. "WASHINGTON & INDEPENDENCE."
Rev: Wreath. "UNITY STATES OF AMERICA."

1 Cent 1783 .... 20.00

Obv: Military bust. "WASHINGTON."
Rev: Same bust. "ONE CENT."

1 Cent. No date (1783) **25.00**

Obv: Bust. "WASHINGTON PRESIDENT."
Rev: Large or small eagle. "ONE CENT."

1 Cent 1791 . . . . **60.00**

Obv: Bust. "WASHINGTON PRESIDENT."
Rev: Ship. "LIVERPOOL HALFPENNY."

Half Penny 1791 . . . . **300.00**

Obv: Bust. "WASHINGTON PRESIDENT."
Rev: Large spread eagle. No legend.

1 Cent 1792 .... **Rare**

Obv: Laureate Roman-type head to right. "WASHINGTON PRESIDENT."
Rev: Eagle. "CENT."

1 Cent 1792 .... **Rare**

Obv: Bust. "WASHINGTON PRESIDENT."
Rev: In ten lines, "GENERAL OF THE AMERICAN ARMIES 1775. RESIGNED 1788. PRESIDENT OF THE UNITED STATES 1789."

1 Cent 1792 .... **Rare**

Obv: Bust. "GEO. WASHINGTON BORN VIRGINIA FEBRUARY 11, 1732."
Rev: In ten lines, "GENERAL OF THE AMERICAN ARMIES 1775. RESIGNED 1788. PRESIDENT OF THE UNITED STATES 1789."

1 Cent. No date (1792) **650.00**

Obv: Bust. "G. WASHINGTON PRESIDENT."
Rev: Small eagle, stars above. "UNITED STATES OF AMERICA."

Half Dollar 1792. Struck in silver . . . . —
Half Dollar 1792. Struck in copper . . . . —
Half Dollar 1792. Struck in silver. Similar to above but Rev. has larger eagle and is without stars . . . . —

Obv: Bust. "WASHINGTON PRESIDENT."
Rev: Ship. "HALFPENNY."

Half Penny 1793 . . . . **25.00**

Obv: Bust right. "GEORGE WASHINGTON."
Rev: Eagle over shield. "LIBERTY AND SECURITY 1795."

1 Penny 1795 . . . . **200.00**
Half penny 1795 . . . . **50.00**

Obv: Bust left. "GEORGE WASHINGTON."
Rev: Eagle over shield. "LIBERTY AND SECURITY."

1 Penny. No date (1795) **75.00**

Obv: Bust. "G. WASHINGTON FIRST FRIEND TO PEACE. . . ."
Rev: Grate, legend around edge and "LONDON 1795."

1 Cent 1795. The Grate Cent **40.00**

Obv: Bust. "GEORGE WASHINGTON."
Rev: Circle of fifteen stars. "SUCCESS TO THE UNITED STATES."

Success Token. No date (1795). Large size **50.00**
Success Token. As above but small size **50.00**

Obv: Bust. "GEORGIUS WASHINGTON."
Rev: Crowned harp. "NORTH WALES."

Half Penny. No date (1795) **50.00**

The valuations listed in this book closely approximate how much established coin dealers will pay for any material needed in their stock.

United States Coins

(Complete from 1793 to date)

HALF CENTS

Type: Liberty head with cap facing left.

Date	Amount Minted	Value	Date	Amount Minted	Value
1793	31,900	**700.00**			

Type: Liberty head with cap facing right.

Date	Amount Minted	Value	Date	Amount Minted	Value
1794	81,600	**100.00**	1796	115,500	**1,000.00**
1795	25,600	**80.00**	1797	107,000	**80.00**

Type: Draped bust of Liberty.

Date	Amount Minted	Value	Date	Amount Minted	Value
1800	211,500	**10.00**	1805	814,500	**10.00**
1802	14,400	**90.00**	1806	356,000	**10.00**
1803	97,900	**10.00**	1807	476,000	**10.00**
1804	1 million	**10.00**	1808	400,000	**10.00**

Type: Liberty head in turban.

Date	Amount Minted	Value	Date	Amount Minted	Value
1809	1¼ million	**9.00**	1831 Proof Only	2,200	**4,000.00**
1810	215,000	**17.00**	1832	154,000	**9.00**
1811	63,100	**40.00**	1833	120,000	**9.00**
1825	63,000	**9.00**	1834	141,000	**9.00**
1826	234,000	**9.00**	1835	398,000	**9.00**
1828	606,000	**9.00**	1836 Proof Only	—	**2,750.00**
1829	487,000	**9.00**			

Type: Liberty head with braided hair.

Date	Amount Minted	Value	Date	Amount Minted	Value
1840		**1,500.00**	1849	39,900	**14.00**
1841		**1,500.00**	1850	39,800	**13.00**
1842		**1,500.00**	1851	147,700	**13.00**
1843	Only proofs were	**1,500.00**	1852	Proof only	**1,300.00**
1844	struck of these coins.	**1,500.00**	1853	129,700	**13.00**
1845	The exact quantities	**1,500.00**	1854	55,400	**13.00**
1846	minted are not known.	**1,500.00**	1855	56,500	**13.00**
1847		**1,500.00**	1856	40,400	**15.00**
1848		**1,500.00**	1857	35,200	**17.50**
1849		**1,500.00**			

(The valuations in this book are based on the coins being in G-VG condition, unless otherwise noted.)

LARGE CENTS

Type: Liberty head with close flowing hair; chain on Rev.

Date	*Amount Minted*	*Value*	*Date*	*Amount Minted*	*Value*
1793	—	**1,000.00**		(About 224,000 were coined of all types of 1793 cents)	

Type: Liberty head with loose flowing hair; wreath on Rev.

1793		**425.00**		(See above)	

Type: Liberty head with cap.

1793	(See above)	**600.00**	1795	82,000	**55.00**
1794	918,500	**50.00**	1796	Part of 974,700	**65.00**

Type: Draped bust of Liberty.

Date	*Amount Minted*	*Value*	*Date*	*Amount Minted*	*Value*
1796	Part of 974,700	**35.00**	1802	3½ million	**10.00**
1797	897,500	**16.00**	1803	2½ million	**11.00**
1798	979,700	**15.00**	1804	756,800	**150.00**
1799	904,600	**300.00**	1805	941,100	**11.00**
1800	2¾ million	**12.00**	1806	348,000	**15.00**
1801	1⅓ million	**12.00**	1807	727,200	**11.00**

Type: Liberty head in turban.

1808	1 million	**13.00**	1812	1 million	**13.00**
1809	222,900	**35.00**	1813	418,000	**17.50**
1810	1½ million	**13.00**	1814	357,800	**13.00**
1811	218,000	**17.50**			

Type: Liberty head in coronet.

1816	2¾ million	**4.00**	1818	3¼ million	**2.75**
1817	4 million	**2.75**	1819	2⅔ million	**2.75**

Date	*Amount Minted*	*Value*	*Date*	*Amount Minted*	*Value*
1820	4½ million	**2.75**	1830	1¾ million	**2.75**
1821	389,000	**10.00**	1831	3⅓ million	**2.75**
1822	2 million	**2.75**	1832	2⅓ million	**2.75**
1823	855,700	**20.00**	1833	2¾ million	**2.50**
1824	1½ million	**2.75**	1834	2 million	**2.75**
1825	1½ million	**2.75**	1835	Part of 4 million	**2.50**
1826	1½ million	**2.75**	1836	2 million	**2.50**
1827	2⅓ million	**2.75**	1837	5½ million	**2.50**
1828	2¼ million	**2.75**	1838	6⅓ million	**2.50**
1829	1½ million	**2.75**	1839	3¼ million	**2.50**

Type: Liberty head with braided hair

Date	*Amount Minted*	*Value*	*Date*	*Amount Minted*	*Value*
1840	2½ million	**2.50**	1849	4¼ million	**2.50**
1841	1½ million	**2.50**	1850	4½ million	**2.50**
1842	2⅓ million	**2.50**	1851	10 million	**2.50**
1843	2½ million	**2.50**	1852	5 million	**2.50**
1844	2½ million	**2.50**	1853	6⅔ million	**2.50**
1845	4 million	**2.50**	1854	4¼ million	**2.50**
1846	4 million	**2.50**	1855	1½ million	**2.50**
1847	6¼ million	**2.50**	1856	2⅔ million	**2.50**
1848	6½ million	**2.50**	1857	333,500	**17.50**

SMALL CENTS

Type: Flying eagle—Copper-Nickel

Date	*Amount Minted*	*Value*	*Date*	*Amount Minted*	*Value*
1856	About 1000	**900.00**	1858	24⅔ million	**5.00**
1857	17½ million	**5.00**			

Type: Indian head; without shield on Rev.—Copper-Nickel

Date	*Amount Minted*	*Value*
1859	36⅓ million	**2.00**

Type: Indian head; with shield on Rev.—Copper-Nickel

Date	*Amount Minted*	*Value*	*Date*	*Amount Minted*	*Value*
1860	20½ million	**2.00**	1863	49¾ million	**1.00**
1861	10 million	**4.00**	1864	13¾ million	**4.00**
1862	28 million	**1.25**			

(The bronze Indian Head Cents which follow are of the same design as the Copper-Nickel Cents above)

Type: Indian head—Bronze

(The "S" mint mark of 1908 and 1909 is on the Rev., under the wreath)

Date	*Amount Minted*	*Value*	*Date*	*Amount Minted*	*Value*
1864	39¼ million	**1.50**	1884	23¼ million	**.85**
1864-L	Part of above	**15.00**	1885	11¾ million	**1.25**
1865	35½ million	**1.50**	1886	17⅔ million	**.60**
1866	9¾ million	**9.00**	1887	45¼ million	**.35**
1867	9¾ million	**9.00**	1888	37½ million	**.35**
1868	10¼ million	**9.00**	1889	48¾ million	**.35**
1869	6½ million	**15.00**	1890	57¼ million	**.35**
1870	5¼ million	**9.00**	1891	47 million	**.35**
1871	4 million	**15.00**	1892	37⅔ million	**.35**
1872	4 million	**20.00**	1893	46⅔ million	**.35**
1873	11⅔ million	**4.00**	1894	16¾ million	**.65**
1874	14¼ million	**4.00**	1895	38⅓ million	**.25**
1875	13½ million	**4.00**	1896	39 million	**.25**
1876	8 million	**7.00**	1897	50½ million	**.25**
1877	852,500	**100.00**	1898	49¾ million	**.25**
1878	5¾ million	**7.50**	1899	53⅔ million	**.25**
1879	16¼ million	**1.25**	1900	66¾ million	**.20**
1880	39 million	**.70**	1901	79⅔ million	**.20**
1881	39¼ million	**.70**	1902	87⅓ million	**.20**
1882	38½ million	**.70**	1903	85 million	**.20**
1883	45½ million	**.70**	1904	61⅓ million	**.20**

Date	*Amount Minted*	*Value*	*Date*	*Amount Minted*	*Value*
1905	80¾ million	**.20**	1908-S	1 million	**8.00**
1906	96 million	**.20**	1909	14⅓ million	**.50**
1907	108¼ million	**.20**	1909-S	309,000	**50.00**
1908	32⅓ million	**.20**			

Type: Lincoln head

(The mint mark is on the Obv., under the date)

Date	*Amount Minted*	*Value*	*Date*	*Amount Minted*	*Value*
1909-VDB	28 million	**.75**	1919	392 million	**.03**
1909-S-VDB	484,000	**150.00**	1919-D	57¼ million	**.07**
1909	72¾ million	**.15**	1919-S	139¾ million	**.07**
1909-S	1¾ million	**20.00**	1920	310¼ million	**.03**
1910	146¾ million	**.05**	1920-D	49⅓ million	**.05**
1910-S	6 million	**3.00**	1920-S	46¼ million	**.05**
1911	101¼ million	**.05**	1921	39¼ million	**.05**
1911-D	12¾ million	**1.50**	1921-S	15⅓ million	**.30**
1911-S	4 million	**5.00**	1922-D	7¼ million	**1.50**
1912	68¼ million	**.05**	1922	Plain Part of above	**70.00**
1912-D	10½ million	**1.50**	1923	74¾ million	**.03**
1912-S	4½ million	**4.50**	1923-S	8¾ million	**.50**
1913	76½ million	**.05**	1924	75¼ million	**.03**
1913-D	15¾ million	**.60**	1924-D	2½ million	**4.00**
1913-S	6 million	**2.50**	1924-S	11¾ million	**.25**
1914	75¼ million	**.05**	1925	140 million	**.03**
1914-D	1¼ million	**32.00**	1925-D	22⅔ million	**.05**
1914-S	4 million	**4.00**	1925-S	26½ million	**.05**
1915	29 million	**.20**	1926	157 million	**.03**
1915-D	22 million	**.15**	1926-D	28 million	**.05**
1915-S	4¾ million	**3.00**	1926-S	4⅔ million	**.75**
1916	131¾ million	**.03**	1927	144½ million	**.03**
1916-D	36 million	**.07**	1927-D	27¼ million	**.05**
1916-S	22½ million	**.15**	1927-S	14⅓ million	**.15**
1917	196½ million	**.03**	1928	134 million	**.03**
1917-D	55 million	**.05**	1928-D	31¼ million	**.05**
1917-S	32⅔ million	**.05**	1928-S	17⅓ million	**.10**
1918	288 million	**.02**	1929	185⅓ million	**.03**
1918-D	47¾ million	**.07**	1929-D	41¾ million	**.03**
1918-S	34¾ million	**.07**	1929-S	50 million	**.03**

Date	Amount Minted	Value
1930	157½ million	**.03**
1930-D	40 million	**.03**
1930-S	24⅓ million	**.04**
1931	19½ million	**.10**
1931-S	866,000	**15.00**
1932	9 million	**.40**
1932-D	10½ million	**.20**
1933	14½ million	**.15**
1933-D	6¼ million	**.80**
1934	219 million	**.02**
1934-D	28½ million	**.05**
1935	245½ million	**.02**
1935-D	47 million	**.03**
1935-S	38¾ million	**.03**
1936	309⅔ million	**.02**
1935-D	40⅔ million	**.03**
1936-S	29 million	**.04**
1937	309¼ million	**.02**
1937-D	50½ million	**.03**
1937-S	34½ million	**.04**
1938	156¾ milliion	**.02**
1938-D	20 million	**.05**
1938-S	15¼ million	**.12**
1939	316½ million	**.02**
1939-D	15¼ million	**.12**
1939-S	52 million	**.03**
1940	586¾ million	**.02**
1940-D	81½ million	**.02**
1940-S	113 million	**.02**
1941	887 million	**.02**
1941-D	128¾ million	**.02**
1941-S	92½ million	**.02**
1942	657¾ million	**.02**
1942-D	206¾ million	**.02**
1942-S	85⅔ million	**.02**
1943	684⅔ million	**.02**
1943-D	217¾ million	**.02**
1943-S	191⅔ million	**.03**
1944	1½ billion	**.02**
1944-D	430⅔ million	**.02**
1944-S	232¾ million	**.02**

Date	Amount Minted	Value
1945	1 billion	**.02**
1945-D	226⅓ million	**.02**
1945-S	181¾ million	**.02**
1946	991¾ million	**.02**
1946-D	315¾ million	**.02**
1946-S	198 million	**.02**
1947	190½ million	**.02**
1947-D	194¾ million	**.02**
1947-S	99 million	**.02**
1948	317⅔ million	**.02**
1948-D	172⅔ million	**.02**
1948-S	81¾ million	**.02**
1949	217½ million	**.02**
1949-D	154⅓ million	**.02**
1949-S	64⅓ million	**.02**
1950	272¾ million	**.02**
1950-D	335 million	**.02**
1950-S	118½ million	**.02**
1951	294⅔ million	**.02**
1951-D	625½ million	**.02**
1951-S	101 million	**.02**
1952	187 million	**.02**
1952-D	746 million	**.02**
1952-S	137¾ million	**.02**
1953	257 million	**.02**
1953-D	700½ million	**.02**
1953-S	182 million	**.02**
1954	72 million	**.02**
1954-D	251½ million	**.02**
1954-S	96¼ million	**.02**
1955	331 million	**.02**
1955	double die. (Very Fine)	**200.00**
1955-D	563⅓ million	**.02**
1955-S	44⅔ million	**.10**
1956	421 million	**.02**
1956-D	1 billion	**.02**
1957	282½ million	**.02**
1957-D	1 billion	**.02**
1958	252½ million	**.02**
1958–D	801 million	**.02**

(The valuations in this book are based on the coins being in G-VG condition, unless otherwise noted.)

Type: Lincoln head with the Lincoln Memorial on the reverse

Date	*Amount Minted*	*Value*
1959	609¾ million	**.01**
1959-D	1¼ billion	**.01**
1960	586½ million	**.01**
1960	Small Date (unc)	**1.00**
1960-D	1½ billion	**.01**
1960-D	Small Date	**.02**
1961	753⅓ million	**.01**
1961-D	1¾ billion	**.01**
1962	606 million	**.01**
1962-D	1¾ billion	**.01**
1963	754 million	**.01**
1963-D	1¾ billion	**.01**
1964	2⅔ billion	**.01**
1964-D	3¾ billion	**.01**
1965	1½ billion	**.01**
1966	2¼ billion	**.01**
1967	3 billion	**.01**
1968	1¾ billion	**.01**
1968-D	2¾ billion	**.01**
1968-S	258¼ million	**.01**
1969	1.2 billion	**(unc.).05**
1969-D	4 billion	**.01**
1969-S	544⅓ million	**.01**
1970	1¾ billion	**.01**
1970-D	2¾ billion	**.01**
1970-S	690½ million	**.01**
1970-S	Small Date (unc)	**3.50**
1971	2 billion	**.01**
1971-D	3 billion	**.01**
1971-S	525 million	**.01**
1972	3 billion	**.01**
1972	double die. (unc.)	**100.00**
1972-D	2⅔ billion	**.01**
1972-S	380 million	**.01**
1973	3¾ billion	**.01**
1973-D	3½ billion	**.01**
1973-S	320 million	**.01**
1974	4¼ billion	**.01**
1974-D	4¼ billion	**.01**
1974-S	412 million	**.01**
1975	5½ billion	**.01**
1975-D	4½ billion	**.01**
1975-S	proof only 3 million	**5.00**
1976	4½ billion	**.01**
1976-D	4¼ billion	**.01**
1976-S	proof only 4 million	**1.00**
1977	4½ billion	**.01**
1977-D	4¼ billion	**.01**
1977-S	proof only 3¼ million	**1.00**
1978	5½ billion	**.01**
1978-D	4¼ billion	**.01**
1978-S	proof only 3 million	**1.00**
1979	6 billion	**.01**
1979-D	4¼ billion	**.01**
1979-S	proof only 3¾ million	**1.00**
1980	7½ billion	**.01**
1980-D	5 billion	**.01**
1980-S	proof only 3½ million	**.50**
1981	7½ billion	**.01**
1981-D	5½ billion	**.01**
1981-S	proof only 4 million	**.50**
1982	copper, lg. date	**.02**
1982	copper, sm. date	**.02**
1982	zinc, lg. date	**.01**
1982	zinc, sm. date	**.01**
	(9 billion, all types)	
1982-D	copper, lg. date	**.01**
1982-D	zinc, lg. date	**.05**
1982-D	zinc, sm. date	**.01**
	(6 billion, all types)	
1982-S	3.8 million proofs	**1.00**
1983	7½ billion	**.01**
1983-D	6½ billion	**.01**
1983-S	proof only 3¼ million	**4.00**
1984	8.1 billion	**.01**
1984-D	5.5 billion	**.01**
1984-S	proof only 3 million	**3.75**
1985	5.5 billion	**.01**
1985-D	5.25 billion	**.01**
1985-S	proof only 3.4 million	**3.50**
1986	4.5 billion	**.01**
1986-D	4.4 billion	**.01**
1986-S	proof only 3 million	**3.50**
1987	4.7 billion	**.01**
1987-D	4.9 billion	**.01**
1987-S	proof only	**3.50**
1988		**.01**
1988-D		**.01**
1988-S	proof only	**3.50**

2 CENT PIECES

Type: Bronze with shield on Obv. and the value on the Rev.

Date	*Amount Minted*	*Value*	*Date*	*Amount Minted*	*Value*
1864 Large motto	19¾ million	**1.75**	1869	1½ million	**2.75**
1864 Small motto	Part of above	**30.00**	1870	861,250	**3.00**
1865	13⅔ million	**1.75**	1871	721,250	**4.00**
1866	3¼ million	**2.00**	1872	65,000	**40.00**
1867	3 million	**2.00**	1873	600 proofs	**750.00**
1868	3 million	**2.25**			

3 CENT PIECES—SILVER

Plain star and plain III
1851-1853

Star with borders; sprig and arrows of the III
1854-1873

Type: Large star, the Rev. has the Roman Numeral III for the value.

(The "O" mint mark is on the Rev., to the right of the III)

Date	*Amount Minted*	*Value*	*Date*	*Amount Minted*	*Value*
1851	5½ million	**5.50**	1862	363,550	**6.00**
1851-O	720,000	**7.00**	1863	21,500 proofs	**300.00**
1852	18⅔ million	**5.50**	1864	470 proofs	**300.00**
1853	11½ million	**5.50**	1865	8,500 proofs	**300.00**
1854	671,000	**6.00**	1866	22,700 proofs	**300.00**
1855	139,000	**8.00**	1867	4,625 proofs	**300.00**
1856	1½ million	**5.50**	1868	4,100 proofs	**300.00**
1857	1 million	**5.50**	1869	5,100 proofs	**300.00**
1858	1⅔ million	**5.50**	1870	4,000 proofs	**300.00**
1859	365,000	**6.00**	1871	4,260 proofs	**300.00**
1860	287,000	**6.00**	1872	1,950 proofs	**300.00**
1861	498,000	**6.00**	1873	600 proofs	**600.00**

3 CENT PIECES—NICKEL

Type: Liberty head. The Rev. has the Roman numeral III for the value.

Date	*Amount Minted*	*Value*	*Date*	*Amount Minted*	*Value*
1865	11⅓ million	**2.00**	1878	2,350 proofs	**500.00**
1866	4¾ million	**2.00**	1879	41,200	**25.00**
1867	4 million	**2.00**	1880	25,000	**35.00**
1868	3¼ million	**2.00**	1881	1⅛ million	**2.00**
1869	1⅔ million	**2.00**	1882	25,300	**35.00**
1870	1⅓ million	**2.00**	1883	10,600	**70.00**
1871	604,000	**2.50**	1884	5,650	**150.00**
1872	862,000	**2.50**	1885	4,800	**200.00**
1873	1¼ million	**2.50**	1886	4,300 proofs	**325.00**
1874	790,000	**3.00**	1887	7,960	**100.00**
1875	228,000	**4.00**	1888	41,000	**20.00**
1876	162,000	**4.50**	1889	21,600	**35.00**
1877	510 proofs	**750.00**			

NICKELS

With rays on Rev.
1866-1867

Without rays on Rev.
1867-1883

Type: Shield. The U.S. shield is on the obv. and the value is on the Rev.

Date	*Amount Minted*	*Value*	*Date*	*Amount Minted*	*Value*
1866	14¾ million	**6.00**	1875	2 million	**5.00**
1867	With rays 31 million	**6.50**	1876	2½ million	**5.00**
1867	No rays Part of above	**4.00**	1877	510 proofs	**800.00**
1868	28¾ million	**4.00**	1878	2,350 proofs	**400.00**
1869	16½ million	**4.00**	1879	29,100	**125.00**
1870	4¾ million	**4.50**	1880	19,950	**135.00**
1871	561,000	**13.00**	1881	72,400	**100.00**
1872	6 million	**4.50**	1882	11½ million	**4.00**
1873	4½ million	**4.50**	1883	1½ million	**4.00**
1874	3½ million	**4.50**			

Without "Cents" on Rev.
1883

With "Cents" on Rev.
1883

Type: Liberty head.

(The mint marks of 1912 are on the Rev., to the left of "Cents" and under the dot)

1883 Without "Cents"	5½ million	**1.00**	1890	16¼ million	**2.00**
1883 With "Cents"	16 million	**3.00**	1891	16¾ million	**1.50**
1884	11¼ million	**3.50**	1892	11½ million	**1.60**
1885	1½ million	**90.00**	1893	13⅓ million	**1.50**
1886	3⅓ million	**25.00**	1894	5½ million	**2.25**
1887	15¼ million	**3.00**	1895	10 million	**1.00**
1888	10¾ million	**3.25**	1896	8¾ million	**1.25**
1889	15¾ million	**1.50**	1897	20½ million	**.45**

Date	Amount Minted	Value	Date	Amount Minted	Value
1898	12½ million	**.30**	1909	11½ million	**.20**
1899	26 million	**.30**	1910	30¼ million	**.20**
1900	27¼ million	**.20**	1911	39½ million	**.20**
1901	26½ million	**.20**	1912	26¼ million	**.20**
1902	31½ million	**.20**	1912-D	8½ million	**.30**
1903	28 million	**.20**	1912-S	238,000	**17.50**
1904	21½ million	**.20**	1913	5 pieces struck. All are accounted for in collections and it is not possible to find one.	
1905	29¾ million	**.20**			
1906	38⅔ million	**.20**			
1907	39¼ million	**.20**			
1908	22⅔ million	**.20**			

Type I. Buffalo on hilly mound
1913

Type II. Buffalo on more level mound
1913-1938

Type: Buffalo and Indian head.

(The mint marks are on the Rev., under "Five Cents")

Date	Amount Minted	Value	Date	Amount Minted	Value
1913-I	31 million	**1.50**	1919	60¾ million	**.25**
1913-D-I	5⅓ million	**3.00**	1919-D	8 million	**2.00**
1913-S-I	2 million	**5.00**	1919-S	7½ million	**1.25**
1913-II	29¾ million	**1.25**	1920	63 million	**.20**
1913-D-II	4¼ million	**20.00**	1920-D	9½ million	**1.50**
1913-S-II	1¼ million	**35.00**	1920-S	9⅔ million	**.80**
1914	20⅔ million	**2.00**	1921	10⅔ million	**.30**
1914-D	4 million	**15.00**	1921-S	1½ million	**6.00**
1914-S	3½ million	**2.50**	1923	35¾ million	**.20**
1915	21 million	**.90**	1923-S	6¼ million	**.60**
1915-D	7½ million	**3.25**	1924	21⅔ million	**.15**
1915-S	7½ million	**5.25**	1924-D	5¼ million	**1.00**
1916	63½ million	**.25**	1924-S	1½ million	**2.25**
1916, over 16		**300.00**	1925	35½ million	**.15**
1916-D	13⅓ million	**2.25**	1925-D	4½ million	**1.75**
1916-S	11¾ million	**1.50**	1925-S	6¼ million	**.75**
1917	51½ million	**.20**	1926	44⅔ million	**.10**
1917-D	10 million	**2.25**	1926-D	5⅔ million	**1.00**
1917-S	4¼ million	**1.75**	1926-S	970,000	**2.75**
1918	32 million	**.30**	1927	38 million	**.10**
1918-D	8⅓ million	**2.00**	1927-D	5¾ million	**.40**
1918-D, 8 over 7		**225.00**			
1918-S	4¾ million	**1.50**			

Date	*Amount Minted*	*Value*	*Date*	*Amount Minted*	*Value*
1927-S	3½ million	.25	1935	58¼ million	.10
1928	23½ million	.10	1935-D	12 million	.10
1928-D	6½ million	.25	1935-S	10⅓ million	.10
1928-S	7 million	.25	1936	119 million	.10
1929	36½ million	.10	1936-D	24½ million	.10
1929-D	8⅓ million	.25	1936-S	15 million	.10
1929-S	7¾ million	.12	1937	79½ million	.10
1930	22¾ million	.10	1937-D	17¾ million	.10
1930-S	5½ million	.15	1937-D	3-legged buffalo	40.00
1931-S	1¼ million	1.75	1937-S	5⅔million	.10
1934	20¼ million	.10	1938-D	7 million	.10
1934-D	7½ million	.10			

Normal type
1938-1942 & 1946 to date

Silver content type with large
Mint Mark on Rev.
1942-1945

Type: Jefferson head.

(From 1938-1942 and 1946-1964, the mint marks are on the Rev. to the right of the building. On the silver content nickels, 1942-1945, the mint marks are much larger and are over the building. From 1968 to date, the mint marks are on the obverse under the date.)

Date	Amount Minted	Value	Date	Amount Minted	Value
1938	19½ million	.06	1940-D	43½ million	.05
1938-D	5⅓ million	.35	1940-S	39⅔ million	.05
1938-S	4 million	.75	1941	203¼ million	.05
1939	120⅔ million	.05	1941-D	53½ million	.05
1939-D	3½ million	1.75	1941-S	43½ million	.05
1939-S	6⅔ million	.15	1942	49¾ million	.05
1940	176½ million	.05	1942-D	14 million	.08

Silver content Nickels with large mint mark on reverse.

Date	Amount Minted	Value	Date	Amount Minted	Value
1942-P	56 million	.20	1944-D	32⅓ million	.20
1942-S	33 million	.20	1944-S	21⅔ million	.20
1943-P	27¼ million	.20	1945-P	119½ million	.20
1943-D	15¼ million	.20	1945-D	37¼ million	.20
1943-S	104 million	.20	1945-S	59 million	.20
1944-P	119¼ million	.20			

Standard composition Nickels

(Prices are for uncirculated coins)

Date	Amount Minted	Value	Date	Amount Minted	Value
1946	161 million	.10	1947-D	37¾ million	.25
1946-D	45¼ million	.15	1947-S	24¾ million	.20
1946-S	13⅓ million	.25	1948	89⅓ million	.15
1947	95 million	.10	1948-D	44¾ million	.30

Date	Amount Minted	Value
1948-S	11⅓ million	.25
1949	60⅔ million	.30
1949-D	35¼ million	.30
1949-S	9¾ million	.65
1950	9¾ million	.50
1950-D	2⅔ million	3.50
1951	28⅔ million	.15
1951-D	20½ million	.20
1951-S	7¾ million	.50
1952	64 million	.10
1952-D	30⅔ million	.50
1952-S	20½ million	.20
1953	46¾ million	.07
1953-D	59¾ million	.07
1953-S	19¼ million	.08
1954	48 million	.07
1954-D	117¼ million	.07
1954-S	29⅓ million	.07
1955	8¼ million	.08
1955-D	74½ million	.06
1956	35⅓ million	.05
1956-D	67¼ million	.05
1957	38½ million	.05
1957-D	136¾ million	.05
1958	17 million	.05
1958-D	141¾ million	.05
1959	27¼ million	.05
1959-D	160¾ million	.05
1960	55½ million	.05
1960-D	192½ million	.05
1961	73⅔ million	.05
1961-D	229⅓ million	.05
1962	97⅓ million	.05
1962-D	280¼ million	.05
1963	175¾ million	.05
1963-D	276¾ million	.05
1964	1 billion	.05
1964-D	1¾ billion	.05
1965	136 million	.05
1966	156¼ million	.05
1967	107⅓ million	.05
1968-D	91¼ million	.05
1968-S	100⅓ million	.05
1969-S	120¼ million	.05
1970-D	515½ million	.05
1970-S	238¾ million	.05
1971	106.8 million	.05
1971-D	316 million	.05
1971-S	3¼ million proofs	.35
1972	202 million	.05
1972-D	351⅔ million	.05
1972-S	3¼ million proofs	.35
1973	384⅓ million	.05
1973-D	261⅓ million	.05
1973-S	2¾ million proofs	.35
1974	601¾ million	.05
1974-D	277⅓ million	.05
1974-S	2⅔ million proofs	.50
1975	181¾ million	.05
1975-D	402 million	.05
1975-S	2¾ million proofs	.35
1976	367 million	.05
1976-D	564 million	.05
1976-S	4¼ million proofs	.20
1977	585⅓ million	.05
1977-D	297⅓ million	.05
1977-S	3¼ million proofs	.20
1978	391⅓ million	.05
1978-D	313 million	.05
1978-S	3¼ million proofs	.20
1979	463¼ million	.05
1979-D	325¾ million	.05
1979-S	3⅔ million proofs	.20
1980	600 million	.05
1980-S	3½ million proofs	.20
1981	657½ million	.05
1981-D	364¾ million	.05
1981-S	4 million proofs	.20
1982	292⅓ million	.05
1982-D	373¾ million	.05
1982-S	3.8 million proofs	.40
1983	561½ million	.05
1983-D	536¾ million	.05
1983-S	3¼ million proofs	.75
1984	746 million	.05
1984-D	500 million	.05
1984-S	proof only	1.00
1985	647 million	.05
1985-D	460 million	.05
1985-S	3.3 million proofs	1.00
1986	537 million	.05
1986-D	362 million	.05
1986-S	3 million proofs	.75
1987	371 million	.05
1987-D	411 million	.05
1987-S	proofs	1.00
1988		.05
1988-D		.05
1988-S	proofs	.75

HALF DIMES

Type: Liberty head with flowing hair.

Date	Amount Minted	Value
1794		**400.00**
1795		**350.00**

(The combined coinage of 1794 and 1795 was 86,416 pieces. The exact amount of each year is not known)

Type: Draped bust of Liberty; small eagle on Rev.

Date	Amount Minted	Value
1796	10,200	**400.00**
1797	44,500	**400.00**

Type: Draped bust of Liberty; large eagle on Rev.

Date	Amount Minted	Value
1800	24,000	**300.00**
1801	33,900	**300.00**
1802	13,000	**2,000.00**
1803	37,800	**300.00**
1805	15,600	**320.00**

Type: Bust of Liberty wearing cap.

Date	Amount Minted	Value
1829	1¼ million	**8.00**
1830	1¼ million	**8.00**
1831	1¼ million	**8.00**
1832	965,000	**8.00**
1833	1⅓ million	**8.00**
1834	1½ million	**8.00**
1835	2¾ million	**8.00**
1836	2 million	**8.00**
1837	2¼ million	**8.00**

Type: Liberty seated; no stars on Obv.

(The mint mark is under the value on the Rev.)

Date	Amount Minted	Value
1837	2¼ million	**12.00**
1838-O	70,000	**15.00**

Without arrows at date
1838-1853 & 1856-1859

With arrows at date
1853-1855

Type: Liberty seated; with stars on Obv.

(The mint mark is under the value on the Rev.)

Date	Amount Minted	Value	Date	Amount Minted	Value
1838	2¼ million	**4.00**	1851-O	860,000	**4.50**
1839	1 million	**4.00**	1852	1 million	**2.50**
1839-O	1 million	**5.00**	1852-O	260,000	**15.00**
1840	1⅓ million	**3.00**	1853 No Arr.	*	**15.00**
1840-O	935,000	**5.00**	1853-O No Arr.	*	**75.00**
1841	1¼ million	**2.50**	1853 Arr.	13⅓ million	2.00
1841-O	815,000	**5.00**	1853-O Arr.	2⅓ million	2.00
1842	815,000	**2.50**	1854	5¾ million	2.00
1842-O	350,000	**12.50**	1854-O	1½ million	2.00
1843	1¼ million	**2.50**	1855	1¾ million	2.00
1844	430,000	**3.00**	1855-O	600,000	3.50
1844-O	220,000	**30.00**	1856	4¾ million	2.00
1845	1½ million	**2.50**	1856-O	1 million	2.50
1846	27,000	**75.00**	1857	7¼ million	2.00
1847	1¼ million	**2.50**	1857-O	1⅓ million	2.00
1848	668,000	**3.00**	1858	3½ million	2.00
1848-O	600,000	**3.00**	1858-O	1⅔ million	2.00
1849	1⅓ million	**2.50**	1859	340,000	**5.00**
1849-O	140,000	**15.00**	1859-O	560,000	**5.00**
1850	955,000	**2.50**			
1850-O	690,000	**4.00**			
1851	781,000	**2.75**			

*The figures for the No Arrow coinage are included in the figures for the Arrow coinage.

Type: Liberty seated; with "United States of America" on Obv.

(The mint marks are on the Rev., under or within the wreath)

Date	Amount Minted	Value	Date	Amount Minted	Value
1860	799,000	**2.00**	1863-S	100,000	**6.50**
1860-O	1 million	**2.00**	1864	48,470	**125.00**
1861	3¼ million	**2.00**	1864-S	90,000	**15.00**
1862	1½ million	**2.00**	1865	13,500	**80.00**
1863	18,500	**45.00**	1865-S	120,000	**6.00**

Date	Amount Minted	Value	Date	Amount Minted	Value
1866	10,700	**80.00**	1870	536,600	**4.00**
1866-S	120,000	**6.00**	1871	1½ million	**2.00**
1867	8,600	**100.00**	1871-S	161,000	**6.00**
1867-S	120,000	**6.00**	1872	3 million	**2.00**
1868	85,900	**20.00**	1872-S	837,000	**3.75**
1868-S	280,000	**4.25**	1873	712,600	**3.00**
1869	208,600	**4.00**	1873-S	324,000	**3.50**
1869-S	230,000	**4.00**			

DIMES

Type: Draped bust of Liberty; small eagle on Rev.

1796	22,100	**550.00**	1797	25,300	**500.00**

Type: Draped bust of Liberty; large eagle on Rev.

1798	27,500	**250.00**	1803	33,000	**250.00**
1800	21,800	**250.00**	1804	8,300	**400.00**
1801	34,600	**250.00**	1805	120,800	**200.00**
1802	11,000	**250.00**	1807	165,000	**200.00**

Large Size
1809-1828

Reduced Size
1828-1837

Type: Bust of Liberty wearing cap.

1809	44,700	**25.00**	1811	65,200	**17.50**

Date	Amount Minted	Value	Date	Amount Minted	Value
1814	421,500	**15.00**	1829	770,000	**5.00**
1820	942,600	**7.00**	1830	510,000	**5.00**
1821	1¼ million	**7.00**	1831	771,300	**5.00**
1822	100,000	**50.00**	1832	522,500	**5.00**
1823	440,000	**9.50**	1833	485,000	**5.00**
1824	Unknown	**15.00**	1834	635,000	**5.00**
1825	510,000	**9.00**	1835	1⅓ million	**5.00**
1827	1¼ million	**7.00**	1836	1¼ million	**5.00**
1828	125,000	**15.00**	1837	1 million	**5.00**

Type: Liberty seated; no stars on Obv.

(The mint mark is under the value on the Rev.)

Date	Amount Minted	Value	Date	Amount Minted	Value
1837	Unknown	**12.00**	1838-O	402,400	**15.00**

Without arrows at date
1838-1853 & 1856-1860

With arrows at date
1853-1855

Type: Liberty seated; with stars on Obv.

(The mint mark is under the value on the Rev.)

Date	Amount Minted	Value	Date	Amount Minted	Value
1838	2 million	**4.00**	1846	31,300	**50.00**
1839	1 million	**3.25**	1847	245,000	**3.75**
1839-O	1¼ million	**3.75**	1848	451,500	**3.75**
1840	1⅓ million	**3.00**	1849	839,000	**2.00**
1840-O	1¼ million	**3.75**	1849-O	300,000	**3.75**
1841	1⅔ million	**2.00**	1850	2 million	**2.00**
1841-O	2 million	**2.00**	1850-O	510,000	**2.00**
1842	2 million	**2.00**	1851	1 million	**2.00**
1842-O	2 million	**3.00**	1851-O	400,000	**3.25**
1843	1⅓ million	**2.00**	1852	1½ million	**2.00**
1843-O	150,000	**25.00**	1852-O	430,000	**3.25**
1844	72,500	**25.00**	1853 No Arr.	12¼ million	**20.00**
1845	1¾ million	**2.00**	1853 Arr.		**2.00**
1845-O	230,000	**7.00**	1853-O	1 million	**2.00**

Date	Amount Minted	Value
1854	4½ million	**2.00**
1854-O	1¾ million	**2.00**
1855	2 million	**2.00**
1856	5¾ million	**2.00**
1856-O	1¼ million	**2.00**
1856-S	70,000	**30.00**
1857	5½ million	**2.00**
1857-O	1½ million	**2.00**
1858	1½ million	**2.00**
1858-O	290,000	**3.25**
1858-S	60,000	**30.00**
1859	430,000	**2.00**
1859-O	480,000	**2.00**
1859-S	60,000	**45.00**
1860-S	140,000	**6.00**

Without arrows at date
1860-1873 & 1875-1891

With arrows at date
1873-1874

Type: Liberty seated; with "United States of America" on Obv.

(The mint marks are on the Rev., under or within the wreath)

Date	Amount Minted	Value
1860	607,000	**2.00**
1860-O	40,000	**200.00**
1861	2 million	**1.50**
1861-S	172,500	**8.50**
1862	847,500	**2.00**
1862-S	180,700	**8.50**
1863	14,500	**50.00**
1863-S	157,500	**8.50**
1864	39,000	**75.00**
1864-S	230,000	**6.00**
1865	10,500	**50.00**
1865-S	175,000	**6.00**
1866	8,700	**75.00**
1866-S	135,000	**6.00**
1867	6,600	**125.00**
1867-S	140,000	**6.00**
1868	466,200	**2.00**
1868-S	260,000	**5.00**
1869	256,600	**2.00**
1869-S	450,000	**2.50**
1870	471,500	**2.00**
1870-S	50,000	**30.00**
1871	753,600	**2.00**
1871-S	320,000	**6.00**
1871-CC	20,100	**275.00**
1872	2⅓ million	**1.50**
1872-S	190,000	**7.00**
1872-CC	24,000	**150.00**
1873 No Arr.	1¾ million	**1.50**
1873 Arr.	2¼ million	**4.00**
1873-S	455,000	**7.00**
1873-CC	18,800	**325.00**
1874	3 million	**4.00**
1874-S	240,000	**8.00**
1874-CC	10,800	**600.00**
1875	10⅓ million	**1.50**
1875-S	9 million	**1.50**
1875-CC	4⅔ million	**1.50**
1876	11½ million	**1.50**
1876-S	10½ million	**1.50**
1876-CC	8¼ million	**1.50**
1877	7⅓ million	**1.50**
1877-S	2⅓ million	**1.50**
1877-CC	7¾ million	**1.50**
1878	1⅔ million	**1.50**
1878-CC	200,000	**20.00**
1879	15,100	**95.00**
1880	37,400	**40.00**
1881	25,000	**50.00**
1882	4 million	**1.50**
1883	7⅔ million	**1.50**
1884	3⅓ million	**1.50**
1884-S	565,000	**5.50**
1885	2½ million	**1.50**

Date	Amount Minted	Value	Date	Amount Minted	Value
1885-S	43,700	**100.00**	1889	7⅓ million	**1.50**
1886	6⅓ million	**1.50**	1889-S	972,700	**3.50**
1886-S	206,500	**3.50**	1890	10 million	**1.50**
1887	11¼ million	**1.50**	1890-S	1½ million	**1.50**
1887-S	4½ million	**1.50**	1891	15⅓ million	**1.50**
1888	5½ million	**1.50**	1891-O	4½ million	**1.50**
1888-S	1¾ million	**1.50**	1891-S	3¼ million	**1.50**

Type: Liberty head.

(The mint marks are on the Rev., under the wreath)

Date	Amount Minted	Value	Date	Amount Minted	Value
1892	12 million	**1.00**	1901-S	593,000	**25.00**
1892-O	3¾ million	**2.50**	1902	21⅓ million	**.55**
1892-S	990,700	**17.50**	1902-O	4½ million	**.85**
1893	3⅓ million	**2.50**	1902-S	2 million	**1.50**
1893-O	1¾ million	**9.00**	1903	19½ million	**.55**
1893-S	2½ million	**2.50**	1903-O	8¼ million	**.85**
1894	1⅓ million	**2.75**	1903-S	613,300	**20.00**
1894-O	720,000	**25.00**	1904	14⅔ million	**.55**
1894-S	24	**Rare**	1904-S	800,000	**15.00**
1895	690,900	**40.00**	1905	14½ million	**.55**
1895-O	440,000	**125.00**	1905-O	3½ million	**.85**
1895-S	1 million	**10.00**	1905-S	6¾ million	**.85**
1896	2 million	**2.00**	1906	20 million	**.55**
1896-O	610,000	**30.00**	1906-D	4 million	**.85**
1896-S	575,000	**25.00**	1906-O	2⅔ million	**1.00**
1897	10¾ million	**.55**	1906-S	3¼ million	**.75**
1897-O	666,000	**25.00**	1907	22¼ million	**.55**
1897-S	1⅓ million	**5.00**	1907-D	4 million	**.75**
1898	16⅓ million	**.55**	1907-O	5 million	**.75**
1898-O	2¼ million	**1.50**	1907-S	3¼ million	**1.00**
1898-S	1¾ million	**1.50**	1908	10⅔ million	**.55**
1899	19½ million	**.55**	1908-D	7½ million	**.55**
1899-O	2⅔ million	**1.50**	1908-O	1¾ million	**1.00**
1899-S	1¾ million	**1.50**	1908-S	3¼ million	**.75**
1900	17⅔ million	**.55**	1909	10¼ million	**.55**
1900-O	2 million	**2.00**	1909-D	954,000	**1.25**
1900-S	5¼ million	**.85**	1909-O	2¼ million	**.55**
1901	18¾ million	**.55**	1909-S	1 million	**1.25**
1901-O	5⅔ million	**.85**	1910	11½ million	**.55**

Date	Amount Minted	Value	Date	Amount Minted	Value
1910-D	3½ million	.55	1913-S	510,000	**5.00**
1910-D	1¼ million	.55	1914	17⅓ million	.55
1911	19 million	.55	1914-D	12 million	.55
1911-D	11¼ million	.55	1914-S	2 million	.85
1911-S	3½ million	.55	1915	5⅔ million	.55
1912	19⅓ million	.55	1915-S	960,000	.75
1912-D	11¾ million	.55	1916	18½ million	.55
1912-S	3⅓ million	.55	1916-S	5¾ million	.55
1913	19¾ million	.55			

Type: Mercury head.

(The mint marks are on the bottom of the Rev. to the left of the branches)

Date	Amount Minted	Value	Date	Amount Minted	Value
1916	22¼ million	**1.00**	1926-S	1½ million	**2.75**
1916-D	264,000	**250.00**	1927	28 million	.50
1916-S	10½ million	**1.25**	1927-D	4¾ million	**1.00**
1917	55¼ million	.75	1927-S	4¾ million	.75
1917-D	9⅓ million	.85	1928	19½ million	.50
1917-S	27⅓ million	.75	1928-D	4¼ million	.75
1918	26⅔ million	.50	1928-S	7⅓ million	.75
1918-D	22⅔ million	.50	1929	26 million	.50
1918-S	19⅓ million	.75	1929-D	5 million	.75
1919	35¾ million	.75	1929-S	4¾ million	.75
1919-D	10 million	**1.25**	1930	6¾ million	.75
1919-S	8¾ million	**1.00**	1930-S	1¾ million	**1.25**
1920	59 million	.50	1931	3¼ million	.75
1920-D	19¼ million	.75	1931-D	1¼ million	**2.25**
1920-S	13¾ million	.75	1931-S	1¾ million	**1.00**
1921	1¼ million	**15.00**	1934	24 million	.45
1921-D	1 million	**20.00**	1934-D	6¾ million	.45
1923	50¼ million	.50	1935	58¾ million	.45
1923-S	6½ million	**1.00**	1935-D	10½ million	.45
1924	24 million	.50	1935-S	15¾ million	.45
1924-D	6¾ million	.75	1936	87½ million	.45
1924-S	7 million	.75	1936-D	16¼ million	.45
1925	25⅔ million	.50	1936-S	9¼ million	.45
1925-D	5 million	**1.50**	1937	56¾ million	.45
1925-S	5¾ million	.75	1937-D	14¼ million	.45
1926	32¼ million	.50	1937-S	9¾ million	.45
1926-D	6¾ million	.75	1938	22¼ million	.45

(The valuations in this book are based on the coins being in G-VG condition, unless otherwise noted.)

Date	Amount Minted	Value	Date	Amount Minted	Value
1938-D	5½ million	.45	1942/1		80.00
1938-S	8 million	.45	1942-D	60¾ million	.45
1939	67¾ million	.45	1942-S	49⅓ million	.45
1939-D	24⅓ million	.45	1943	191¾ million	.45
1939-S	10½ million	.45	1943-D	72 million	.45
1940	65⅓ million	.45	1943-S	60⅓ million	.45
1940-D	21¼ million	.45	1944	231½ million	.45
1940-S	21½ million	.45	1944-D	62¼ million	.45
1941	175 million	.45	1944-S	49½ million	.45
1941-D	45⅔ million	.45	1945	159¼ million	.45
1941-S	43 million	.45	1945-D	40¼ million	.45
1942	205½ million	.45	1945-S	42 million	.45

Type: Roosevelt head.

(From 1946-1964, the mint marks are on the Rev., at left bottom of torch. From 1968 to date, the mint marks are on the obverse above the date.)

Date	Amount Minted	Value	Date	Amount Minted	Value
1946	255¼ million	.45	1955-D	14 million	.45
1946-D	61 million	.50	1955-S	18½ million	.45
1946-S	28 million	.50	1956	108¾ million	.45
1947	121½ million	.45	1956-D	108 million	.45
1947-D	46¾ million	.50	1957	160¼ million	.45
1947-S	34¾ million	.50	1957-D	113⅓ million	.45
1948	75 million	.45	1958	32 million	.45
1948-D	52¾ million	.50	1958-D	136½ million	.45
1948-S	35½ million	.50	1959	85¾ million	.45
1949	31 million	.50	1959-D	165 million	.45
1949-D	26 million	.50	1960	72 million	.45
1949-S	13½ million	.75	1960-D	200¼ million	.45
1950	50¼ million	.45	1961	93¾ million	.45
1950-D	46¾ million	.45	1961-D	209¼ million	.45
1950-S	20½ million	.45	1962	72½ million	.45
1951	104 million	.45	1962-D	353¼ million	.45
1951-D	52¼ million	.45	1963	123⅔ million	.45
1951-S	31⅔ million	.45	1963-D	421½ million	.45
1952	92¼ million	.45	1964	929⅓ million	.45
1952-D	122 million	.45	1964-D	1⅓ billion	.45
1952-S	44½ million	.45			
1953	53⅔ million	.45			
1953-D	136½ million	.45		**CLAD COINAGE**	
1953-S	39¼ million	.45	1965	1⅔ billion	.10
1954	114¼ million	.45	1966	1⅓ billion	.10
1954-D	106⅓ million	.45	1967	2¼ billion	.10
1954-S	22¾ million	.45	1968	424½ million	.10
1955	12¾ million	.45	1968-D	480¾ million	.10

Date	Amount Minted	Value
1968-S	3 million proofs	**.20**
1969	145¾ million	**.10**
1969-D	563⅓ million	**.10**
1969-S	3 million proofs	**.20**
1970	345½ million	**.10**
1970-D	755 million	**.10**
1970-S	2½ million proofs	**.30**
1971	162⅔ million	**.10**
1971-D	378 million	**.10**
1971-S	3¼ million proofs	**.30**
1972	431½ million	**.10**
1972-D	330¼ million	**.10**
1972-S	3¼ million proofs	**.30**
1973	315⅔ million	**.10**
1973-D	455 million	**.10**
1973-S	2¾ million	**.40**
1974	470¼ million	**.10**
1974-D	571 million	**.10**
1974-S	2⅔ million proofs	**.25**
1975	585¾ million	**.10**
1975-D	313¾ million	**.10**
1975-S	2¾ million proofs	**.30**
1976	568¾ million	**.10**
1976-D	695¼ million	**.10**
1976-S	4¼ million proofs	**.20**
1977	797 million	**.10**
1977-D	376½ million	**.10**
1977-S	3¼ million proofs	**.20**
1978	664 million	**.10**
1978-D	282¾ million	**.10**
1978-S	3¼ million proofs	**.25**
1979	315½ million	**.10**
1979-D	391 million	**.10**
1979-S	3¾ million proofs	**.25**
1980	73.5 million	**.10**
1980-D	719⅓ million	**.10**
1980-S	3½ million proofs	**.20**
1981	676⅔ million	**.10**
1981-D	712¼ million	**.10**
1981-S	4 million proofs	**.25**
1982	519½ million	**.10**
1982-D	542¾ million	**.10**
1982-S	3¾ million proofs	**.25**
1983	647 million	**.10**
1983-D	730 million	**.10**
1983-S	3¾ million proofs	**.50**
1984	856½ million	**.10**
1984-D	700 million	**.10**
1984-S	3 million proofs	**.40**
1985	705 million	**.10**
1985-D	588 million	**.10**
1985-S	3.4 million proofs only	**.40**
1986	683 million	**.10**
1986-D	473 million	**.10**
1986-S	3 million proofs	**.30**
1987	763 million	**.10**
1987-D	653 million	**.10**
1987-S	proofs	**.40**
1988		**.10**
1988-D		**.10**
1988-S	proofs	**.40**

20 CENT PIECES

Type: Liberty seated.

(The mint marks are on the Rev., under the eagle)

Date	Amount Minted	Value
1875	39,700	**25.00**
1875-S	1⅛ million	**20.00**
1875-CC	133,300	**27.00**
1876	15,900	**35.00**
1876-CC	10,000*	**Rare**
1877	510 proofs	**1,900.00**
1878	600 proofs	**1,800.00**

*About a dozen are actually known.

QUARTERS

Type: Draped bust of Liberty; small eagle on Rev.

Date	*Amount Minted*	*Value*
1796	5,900	**2,500.00**

Type: Draped bust of Liberty; large eagle on Rev.

Date	*Amount Minted*	*Value*
1804	6,700	**350.00**
1805	121,400	**100.00**
1806	206,100	**100.00**
1807	220,600	**100.00**

Type: Bust of Liberty wearing cap; motto over the eagle.

Date	Amount Minted	Value	Date	Amount Minted	Value
1815	69,200	**20.00**	1823	17,800	**1,500.00**
1818	361,200	**20.00**	1824	Unknown	**20.00**
1819	144,000	**20.00**	1825	168,000	**20.00**
1820	127,400	**20.00**	1827	4,000	**Rare**
1821	216,900	**20.00**	1828	102,000	**20.00**
1822	64,000	**20.00**			

Type: Bust of Liberty wearing cap; without motto over the eagle.

Date	Amount Minted	Value	Date	Amount Minted	Value
1831	398,000	**17.50**	1835	2 million	**17.50**
1832	320,000	**17.50**	1836	472,000	**17.50**
1833	156,000	**17.50**	1837	252,400	**17.50**
1834	286,000	**17.50**	1838	Part of 832,000	**17.50**

Without arrows or rays
1838-1853 & 1856-1865

With arrows and rays 1853 only
With arrows only, 1854-1855

Type: Liberty seated; without motto over the eagle.

(The mint marks are on the Rev., under the eagle)

Date	*Amount Minted*	*Value*	*Date*	*Amount Minted*	*Value*
1838	Part of 832,000	**5.50**	1854-O	1½ million	**3.50**
1839	491,000	**5.50**	1855	2¾ million	**3.50**
1840	188,127	**10.00**	1855-O	176,000	**30.00**
1840-O	425,200	**6.50**	1855-S	396,400	**30.00**
1841	120,000	**17.50**	1856	7¼ million	**3.50**
1841-O	452,000	**5.00**	1856-O	968,000	**3.50**
1842	88,000	**40.00**	1856-S	286,000	**15.00**
1842-O	769,000	**4.00**	1857	9⅔ million	**3.50**
1843	645,600	**4.00**	1857-O	1¼ million	**3.50**
1843-O	968,000	**4.00**	1857-S	82,000	**30.00**
1844	421,200	**4.00**	1858	7⅓ million	**3.50**
1844-O	740,000	**4.00**	1858-O	520,000	**3.50**
1845	922,000	**4.00**	1858-S	121,000	**20.00**
1846	510,000	**4.00**	1859	1⅓ million	**3.50**
1847	734,000	**4.00**	1859-O	260,000	**5.00**
1847-O	368,000	**12.00**	1859-S	80,000	**40.00**
1848	146,000	**12.00**	1860	805,400	**3.50**
1849	340,000	**10.00**	1860-O	388,000	**3.50**
1849-O	Unknown	**225.00**	1860-S	56,000	**60.00**
1850	190,800	**4.00**	1861	4¾ million	**3.50**
1850-O	412,000	**15.00**	1861-S	96,000	**12.00**
1851	160,000	**4.00**	1862	932,600	**3.50**
1851-O	88,000	**90.00**	1862-S	67,000	**15.00**
1852	177,100	**12.00**	1863	192,100	**10.00**
1852-O	96,000	**150.00**	1864	94,100	**15.00**
1853 Arr. & Rays	15¼ million	**4.00**	1864-S	20,000	**75.00**
1853/3 No Arr.	Part of above	**100.00**	1865	59,300	**27.50**
1853-O	1⅓ million	**4.00**	1865-S	41,000	**27.50**
1854	12⅓ million	**3.50**			

(The valuations in this book are based on the coins being in G-VG condition, unless otherwise noted.)

Without arrows at date
1866-1873 & 1875-1891

With arrows at date
1873-1874

Type: Liberty seated; with motto over the eagle.

(The mint marks are on the Rev., under the eagle)

Date	*Amount Minted*	*Value*	*Date*	*Amount Minted*	*Value*
1866	17,500	**125.00**	1876	17¾ million	**3.00**
1866-S	28,000	**60.00**	1876-S	8½ million	**3.00**
1867	20,600	**60.00**	1876-CC	5 million	**3.00**
1867-S	48,000	**32.50**	1877	11 million	**3.00**
1868	30,000	**35.00**	1877-S	9 million	**3.00**
1868-S	96,000	**25.00**	1877-CC	4¼ million	**3.00**
1869	16,600	**60.00**	1878	2¼ million	**3.00**
1869-S	76,000	**25.00**	1878-S	140,000	**20.00**
1870	87,400	**17.50**	1878-CC	996,000	**6.00**
1870-CC	8,300	**750.00**	1879	14,700	**40.00**
1871	171,200	**3.50**	1880	15,000	**40.00**
1871-S	30,900	**100.00**	1881	13,000	**40.00**
1871-CC	10,900	**350.00**	1882	16,300	**40.00**
1872	182,900	**3.50**	1883	15,400	**40.00**
1872-S	83,000	**75.00**	1884	8,900	**45.00**
1872-CC	9,100	**150.00**	1885	14,500	**40.00**
1873-No Arr.	143,700	**4.00**	1886	5,900	**75.00**
1873-CC-No. Arr.	4,000	**Rare**	1887	10,700	**40.00**
1873-Arr.	1⅓ million	**3.50**	1888	10,800	**40.00**
1873-S.Arr.	156,000	**8.00**	1888-S	1¼ million	**3.00**
1873-CC-Arr.	12,500	**275.00**	1889	12,700	**40.00**
1874	471,900	**8.00**	1890	80,600	**20.00**
1874-S	392,000	**8.00**	1891	4 million	**3.00**
1875	4¼ million	**3.00**	1891-O	68,000	**75.00**
1875-S	680,000	**4.00**	1891-S	2¼ million	**3.00**
1875-CC	140,000	**20.00**			

Type: Liberty head.

(The mint marks are on the Rev., under the eagle)

Date	*Amount Minted*	*Value*	*Date*	*Amount Minted*	*Value*
1892	8¼ million	**1.25**	1892-S	964,100	**9.00**
1892-O	2⅔ million	**2.25**	1893	5½ million	**1.25**

Date	Amount Minted	Value	Date	Amount Minted	Value
1893-O	3½ million	**1.50**	1905-O	1¼ million	**2.00**
1893-S	1½ million	**2.00**	1905-S	1¾ million	**2.00**
1894	3½ million	**1.50**	1906	3⅔ million	**1.15**
1894-O	2¾ million	**1.75**	1906-D	3⅓ million	**1.25**
1894-S	2⅔ million	**1.75**	1906-O	2 million	**1.25**
1895	4½ million	**1.25**	1907	7¼ million	**1.15**
1895-O	2¾ million	**1.75**	1907-D	2½ million	**1.25**
1895-S	1¾ million	**1.90**	1907-O	4½ million	**1.25**
1896	3¾ million	**1.50**	1907-S	1⅓ million	**1.90**
1896-O	1½ million	**2.00**	1908	4¼ million	**1.15**
1896-S	188,000	**100.00**	1908-D	5¾ million	**1.25**
1897	8 million	**1.15**	1908-O	6¼ million	**1.25**
1897-O	1½ million	**3.00**	1908-S	784,000	**3.00**
1897-S	542,200	**4.00**	1909	9¼ million	**1.15**
1898	11 million	**1.15**	1909-D	5 million	**1.25**
1898-O	1¾ million	**2.00**	1909-O	712,000	**4.00**
1898-S	1 million	**2.00**	1909-S	1⅓ million	**1.25**
1899	12⅔ million	**1.15**	1910	2¼ million	**1.15**
1899-O	2⅔ million	**1.90**	1910-D	1½ million	**1.15**
1899-S	708,000	**3.00**	1911	3¾ million	**1.15**
1900	10 million	**1.15**	1911-D	933,600	**1.25**
1900-O	3½ million	**2.25**	1911-S	988,000	**1.25**
1900-S	1¾ million	**2.25**	1912	4½ million	**1.15**
1901	9 million	**1.15**	1912-S	708,000	**1.15**
1901-O	1⅔ million	**5.50**	1913	484,600	**4.50**
1901-S	72,700	**500.00**	1913-D	1½ million	**1.25**
1902	12¼ million	**1.15**	1913-S	40,000	**125.00**
1902-O	4¾ million	**1.90**	1914	6¼ million	**1.25**
1902-S	1½ million	**3.50**	1914-D	3 million	**1.25**
1903	9⅔ million	**1.15**	1914-S	264,000	**6.50**
1903-O	3½ million	**1.90**	1915	3½ million	**1.15**
1903-S	1 million	**3.25**	1915-D	3¾ million	**1.25**
1904	9½ million	**1.15**	1915-S	704,000	**1.90**
1904-O	2½ million	**1.90**	1916	1¾ million	**1.15**
1905	5 million	**1.15**	1916-D	6½ million	**1.25**

Type I. No stars under eagle
1916–1917

Type II. Three stars under eagle
1917–1930

Type: Liberty standing

(The mint marks are on the Obv., above and to left of the date)

Date	Amount Minted	Value	Date	Amount Minted	Value
1916	52,000	**650.00**	1917-II	14 million	**7.50**
1917-I	8¾ million	**5.00**	1917-D-II	6¼ million	**11.50**
1917-D-I	1½ million	**9.00**	1917-S-II	5½ million	**11.00**
1917-S-I	2 million	**9.00**	1918	14¼ million	**8.00**

Date	*Amount Minted*	*Value*
1918-D	7⅓ million	**12.50**
1918-S	11 million	**10.00**
1918-S over 17	—	**750.00**
1919	11⅓ million	**13.00**
1919-D	2 million	**25.00**
1919-S	1¾ million	**25.00**
1920	28 million	**8.50**
1920-D	3½ million	**14.00**
1920-S	6⅓ million	**9.00**
1921	2 million	**30.00**
1923	9¾ million	**9.00**
1923-S	1⅓ million	**65.00**
1924	11 million	**7.00**
1924-D	3 million	**12.50**
1924-S	3 million	**9.00**

Date	*Amount Minted*	*Value*
1925	12¼ million	**1.25**
1926	11¼ million	**1.25**
1926-D	1¾ million	**3.00**
1926-S	2¾ million	**1.75**
1927	12 million	**1.25**
1927-D	976,400	**2.50**
1927-S	396,000	**4.00**
1928	6⅓ million	**1.25**
1928-D	1⅔ million	**1.50**
1928-S	2⅔ million	**1.25**
1929	11 million	**1.25**
1929-D	1⅓ million	**1.25**
1929-S	1¾ million	**1.25**
1930	5⅔ million	**1.25**
1930-S	1⅔ million	**1.25**

Reg. Obv.
1932–1974

Reg. Rev.
1932–1974

Bicentennial
Obv.—1976

Bicentennial
Rev.—1976

Type: Washington head

(From 1932–1964, the mint marks are on the Rev., under the eagle. From 1968 to date, the mint marks are on the obverse, to the right of Washington's neck)

Date	*Amount Minted*	*Value*
1932	5½ million	**1.25**
1932-D	436,800	**20.00**
1932-S	408,000	**17.50**
1934	32 million	**1.15**
1934-D	3½ million	**1.15**
1935	32½ million	**1.15**
1935-D	5¾ million	**1.15**
1935-S	5¾ million	**1.15**
1936	41⅓ million	**1.15**
1936-D	5½ million	**1.25**
1936-S	3¾ million	**1.15**
1937	19¾ million	**1.15**
1937-D	7¼ million	**1.15**
1937-S	1¾ million	**1.75**
1938	9½ million	**1.15**
1938-S	2¾ million	**1.15**
1939	33½ million	**1.15**
1939-D	7 million	**1.15**
1939-S	2⅔ million	**1.15**
1940	35¾ million	**1.15**
1940-D	2¾ million	**1.15**

Date	*Amount Minted*	*Value*
1940-S	8¼ million	**1.15**
1941	79 million	**1.15**
1941-D	16¾ million	**1.15**
1941-S	16 million	**1.15**
1942	102 million	**1.15**
1942-D	17½ million	**1.15**
1942-S	19½ million	**1.15**
1943	99¾ million	**1.15**
1943-D	16 million	**1.15**
1943-S	21¾ million	**1.15**
1944	105 million	**1.15**
1944-D	14⅔ million	**1.15**
1944-S	12⅔ million	**1.15**
1945	74½ million	**1.15**
1945-D	12⅓ million	**1.15**
1945-S	17 million	**1.15**
1946	53½ million	**1.15**
1946-D	9 million	**1.15**
1946-S	4¼ million	**1.15**
1947	22⅔ million	**1.15**
1947-D	15⅓ million	**1.15**

Date	Amount Minted	Value	Date	Amount Minted	Value
1947-S	5½ million	**1.15**	1971	109¼ million	**.25**
1948	35¼ million	**1.15**	1971-D	258⅔ million	**.25**
1948-D	16¾ million	**1.15**	1971-S	3¼ million proofs	**.35**
1948-S	16 million	**1.15**	1972	215 million	**.25**
1949	9⅓ million	**1.15**	1972-D	311 million	**.25**
1949-D	10 million	**1.15**	1972-S	3¼ million proofs	**.35**
1950	25 million	**1.15**	1973	347 million	**.25**
1950-D	21 million	**1.15**	1973-D	233 million	**.25**
1950-S	10⅓ million	**1.15**	1973-S	2¾ million proofs	**.30**
1951	43½ million	**1.15**	1974	801½ million	**.25**
1951-D	35½ million	**1.15**	1974-D	353¼ million	**.25**
1951-S	9 million	**1.15**	1974-S	2⅔ million proofs	**.30**
1952	39 million	**1.15**	1975	none minted	—
1952-D	49¾ million	**1.15**	1976	809¾ million	**.25**
1952-S	13¾ million	**1.15**	1976-D	860 million	**.25**
1953	18¾ million	**1.15**	1976-S	cupro-nickel, proof, 7	**.30**
1953-D	56 million	**1.15**	1976-S	silver	**.75**
1953-S	14 million	**1.15**	1976-S	silver, proof	**1.25**
1954	54⅔ million	**1.15**	1977	468½ million	**.25**
1954-D	46⅓ million	**1.15**	1977-D	256½ million	**.25**
1954-S	11¾ million	**1.15**	1977-S	3¼ million proofs	**.30**
1955	18⅔ million	**1.15**	1978	521½ million	**.25**
1955-D	3¼ million	**1.15**	1978-D	287¼ million	**.25**
1956	44⅓ million	**1.15**	1978-S	3¼ million proofs	**.30**
1956-D	32⅓ million	**1.15**	1979	515¾ million	**.25**
1957	46½ million	**1.15**	1979-D	489¾ million	**.25**
1957-D	78 million	**1.15**	1979-S	3¾ million proofs	**.30**
1958	6⅓ million	**1.15**	1980	635¾ million	**.25**
1958-D	78¼ million	**1.15**	1980-D	518⅓ million	**.25**
1959	24⅓ million	**1.15**	1980-S, proof	3½ million proofs	**.30**
1959-D	62 million	**1.15**	1981	601¾ million	**.25**
1960	30¾ million	**1.15**	1981-D	575¾ million	**.25**
1960-D	63 million	**1.15**	1981-S	4 million proofs	**.30**
1961	37 million	**1.15**	1982	501 million	**.25**
1961-D	80¼ million	**1.15**	1982-D	480 million	**.25**
1962	36¼ million	**1.15**	1982-S	3.8 million proofs	**.30**
1962-D	127½ million	**1.15**	1983	673½ million	**.25**
1963	74⅓ million	**1.15**	1983-D	618 million	**.25**
1963-D	135¼ million	**1.15**	1983-S	3.8 million proofs	**.40**
1964	560⅓ million	**1.15**	1984	673½ million	**.25**
1964	704 million	**1.15**	1984-D	546½ million	**.25**
	CLAD COINAGE		1984-S	proofs	**.35**
1965	1¾ billion	**.25**	1985	776 million	**.25**
1966	821 million	**.25**	1985-D	520 million	**.25**
1967	1½ billion	**.25**	1985-S	3.4 million proofs	**.35**
1968	220¾ million	**.25**	1986	551 million	**.25**
1968-D	101½ million	**.25**	1986-D	504 million	**.25**
1968-S	3 million proofs	**.30**	1986-S	3 million proofs	**.40**
1969	176¼ million	**.25**	1987		**.25**
1969-D	114⅓ million	**.25**	1987-D		**.25**
1969-S	3 million proofs	**.35**	1987-S	proofs	**.50**
1970	136½ million	**.25**	1988		**.25**
1970-D	417⅓ million	**.25**	1988-D		**.25**
1970-S	2½ million proofs	**.35**	1988-S	proofs	**.50**

HALF DOLLARS

Type: Liberty head with flowing hair.

Date	*Amount Minted*	*Value*	*Date*	*Amount Minted*	*Value*
1794	5,300	**275.00**	1795	317,800	**240.00**

Type: Draped bust of Liberty; small eagle on Rev.

Date	Amount Minted	Value	Date	Amount Minted	Value
1796	Unknown	**6,000.00**	1797		**6,000.00**

Type: Draped bust of Liberty; large eagle on Rev.

Date	Amount Minted	Value	Date	Amount Minted	Value
1801	30,300	**85.00**	1805	211,700	**40.00**
1802	29,900	**50.00**	1806	839,600	**35.00**
1803	31,700	**45.00**	1807	301,100	**35.00**

(The valuations in this book are based on the coins being in G-VG condition, unless otherwise noted.)

Type: Bust of Liberty wearing cap; motto over eagle lettered edge; large size.

Date	Amount Minted	Value	Date	Amount Minted	Value
1807	750,500	**20.00**	1823	1⅔ million	**12.00**
1808	1⅓ million	**17.50**	1824	3½ million	**12.00**
1809	1½ million	**17.50**	1825	3 million	**12.00**
1810	1¼ million	**17.50**	1826	4 million	**12.00**
1811	1¼ million	**17.50**	1827	5½ million	**12.00**
1812	1⅔ million	**17.50**	1828	3 million	**12.00**
1813	1¼ million	**17.50**	1829	3¾ million	**12.00**
1814	1 million	**17.50**	1830	4¾ million	**12.00**
1815	47,100	**135.00**	1831	5¾ million	**12.00**
1817	1¼ million	**16.00**	1832	4¾ million	**12.00**
1818	2 million	**16.00**	1833	5¼ million	**12.00**
1819	2¼ million	**16.00**	1834	6⅓ million	**12.00**
1820	751,100	**20.00**	1835	5⅓ million	**12.00**
1821	1⅓ million	**12.00**	1836	Part of 6½ million	**12.00**
1822	1½ million	**12.00**			

Type: Bust of Liberty wearing cap; no motto over eagle; reeded edge; reduced size; value expressed as "50" cents."

Date	Amount Minted	Value	Date	Amount Minted	Value
1836	Part of 6½ million	**225.00**	1837	3⅔ million	**16.00**

Type: Same as above; but value is expressed as "Half Dol."

(The mint marks are on the Obv., over the date)

Date	Amount Minted	Value	Date	Amount Minted	Value
1838	3½ million	**18.00**	1839	Part of 3⅓ million	**18.00**
1838-O	About 20	**Rare**	1839-O	163,000	**40.00**

Without arrows or rays, 1839-1853 & 1856-1866
With arrows and rays, 1853 only
With arrows only, 1854-1855

Type: Liberty seated; without motto over the eagle.

(The mint marks are on the Rev., under the eagle)

Date	Amount Minted	Value	Date	Amount Minted	Value
1839	Part of 3⅓ million	**14.00**	1847-O	2½ million	**6.00**
1840	1½ million	**15.00**	1848	580,000	**6.00**
1840-O	855,100	**13.00**	1848-O	3¼ million	**6.00**
1841	310,000	**15.00**	1849	1¼ million	**6.00**
1841-O	401,000	**6.00**	1849-O	2⅓ million	**6.00**
1842	2 million	**6.00**	1850	227,000	**30.00**
1842-O	957,000	**6.00**	1850-O	2½ million	**7.00**
1843	3¾ million	**6.00**	1851	200,700	**30.00**
1843-O	2¼ million	**6.00**	1851-O	402,000	**7.00**
1844	1¾ million	**6.00**	1852	77,100	**50.00**
1844-O	2 million	**6.00**	1852-O	144,000	**25.00**
1845	589,000	**6.00**	1853-Arr. & Rays	3½ million	**8.00**
1845-O	2 million	**6.00**	1853-O-No Arr & Rays	1⅓ million	**Rare**
1846	2¼ million	**6.00**	1853-O-Arr. & Rays	Partof above	**8.00**
1846-O	2⅓ million	**6.00**	1854	3 million	**7.00**
1847	1¼ million	**6.00**	1854-O	5¼ million	**7.00**

Date	Amount Minted	Value	Date	Amount Minted	Value
1855	759,500	**7.00**	1860	303,700	**10.00**
1855-O	3⅔ million	**7.00**	1860-O	1¼ million	**6.00**
1855-S	129,900	**150.00**	1860-S	472,000	**6.00**
1856	938,000	**6.00**	1861	2¾ million	**6.00**
1856-O	2⅔ million	**6.00**	1861-O	2½ million	**6.00**
1856-S	211,000	**12.00**	1861-S	939,500	**6.00**
1857	2 million	**6.00**	1862	252,300	**10.00**
1857-O	818,000	**6.00**	1862-S	1⅓ million	**6.00**
1857-S	158,000	**15.00**	1863	503,700	**10.00**
1858	4¼ million	**6.00**	1863-S	916,000	**6.00**
1858-O	7¼ million	**6.00**	1864	379,600	**10.00**
1858-S	476,000	**9.00**	1864-S	658,000	**6.00**
1859	748,000	**6.00**	1865	511,900	**10.00**
1859-O	2¾ million	**6.00**	1865-S	675,000	**6.00**
1859-S	566,000	**9.00**	1866-S	Part of 1 million	**25.00**

Without arrows at date, 1866-1873 & 1875-1891
With arrows at date, 1873-1874

Type: Liberty seated; with motto over the eagle.

(The mint marks are on the Rev., under the eagle)

Date	Amount Minted	Value	Date	Amount Minted	Value
1866	745,600	**5.00**	1872-S	580,000	**5.00**
1866-S	Part of 1 million	**5.00**	1872-CC	272,000	**30.00**
1867	424,300	**10.00**	1873-No Arr.	820,800	**5.00**
1867-S	1¼ million	**5.00**	1873-CC-No Arr.	122,500	**30.00**
1868	378,200	**12.00**	1873-Arr.	1¾ million	**12.50**
1868-S	1¼ million	**5.00**	1873-S-Arr.	228,000	**15.00**
1869	795,900	**5.00**	1873-CC-Arr.	214,600	**22.50**
1869-S	656,000	**5.00**	1874	2⅓ million	**12.50**
1870	600,900	**5.00**	1874-S	394,000	**15.00**
1870-S	1 million	**5.00**	1874-CC	59,000	**75.00**
1870-CC	54,600	**200.00**	1875	6 million	**5.00**
1871	1¼ million	**5.00**	1875-S	3¼ million	**5.00**
1871-S	2¼ million	**5.00**	1875-CC	1 million	**7.00**
1871-CC	139,900	**50.00**	1876	8½ million	**5.00**
1872	881,500	**5.00**	1876-S	4½ million	**5.00**

Date	*Amount Minted*	*Value*	*Date*	*Amount Minted*	*Value*
1876-CC	2 million	**5.00**	1882	5,500	**75.00**
1877	8⅓ million	**5.00**	1883	9,000	**70.00**
1877-S	5⅓ million	**5.00**	1884	5,300	**75.00**
1877-CC	1½ million	**5.00**	1885	6,100	**75.00**
1878	1⅓ million	**5.00**	1886	5,900	**75.00**
1878-S	12,000	**1,250.00**	1887	5,700	**75.00**
1878-CC	62,000	**100.00**	1888	12,800	65.00
1879	5,900	**75.00**	1889	12,700	**65.00**
1880	9,800	**70.00**	1890	12,600	**65.00**
1881	11,000	**70.00**	1891	200,600	**10.00**

Type: Liberty Head.

(The mint marks are on the Rev., under the eagle)

Date	Amount Minted	Value	Date	Amount Minted	Value
1892	1 million	**6.00**	1900	4¾ million	**2.50**
1892-O	390,000	**45.00**	1900-O	2¾ million	**3.75**
1892-S	1 million	**50.00**	1900-S	2½ million	**3.75**
1893	1¾ million	**4.00**	1901	4¼ million	**2.50**
1893-O	1⅓ million	**7.00**	1901-O	1 million	**3.75**
1893-S	740,000	**21.00**	1901-S	847,000	**5.00**
1894	1¼ million	**3.75**	1902	5 million	**2.50**
1894-O	2¼ million	**3.75**	1902-O	2½ million	**3.75**
1894-S	4 million	**3.75**	1902-S	1½ million	**3.75**
1895	1¾ million	**3.75**	1903	2¼ million	**2.50**
1895-O	1¾ million	**3.75**	1903-O	2 million	**2.75**
1895-S	1 million	**6.00**	1903-S	2 million	**2.75**
1896	950,800	**3.75**	1904	3 million	**2.50**
1896-O	924,000	**6.00**	1904-O	1 million	**4.00**
1896-S	1¼ million	**20.00**	1904-S	553,000	**5.00**
1897	2½ million	**2.50**	1905	663,000	**4.50**
1897-O	632,000	**20.00**	1905-O	505,000	**5.00**
1897-S	933,900	**40.00**	1905-S	2½ million	**3.00**
1898	3 million	**2.50**	1906	2½ million	**2.50**
1898-O	874,000	**6.00**	1906-D	4 million	**2.50**
1898-S	2⅓ million	**3.75**	1906-O	2½ million	**2.50**
1899	5½ million	**2.50**	1906-S	1¾ million	**2.50**
1899-O	1¾ million	**3.75**	1907	2½ million	**2.50**
1899-S	1½ million	**3.75**	1907-D	3¾ million	**2.50**

Date	Amount Minted	Value	Date	Amount Minted	Value
1907-O	4 million	**2.50**	1911-S	1¼ million	**2.50**
1907-S	1¼ million	**2.50**	1912	1½ million	**2.50**
1908	1⅓ million	**2.50**	1912-D	2⅓ million	**2.50**
1908-D	3¼ million	**2.50**	1912-S	1⅓ million	**2.50**
1908-O	5⅓ million	**2.50**	1913	189,000	**8.00**
1908-S	1⅔ million	**2.50**	1913-D	534,000	**2.50**
1909	2⅓ million	**2.50**	1913-S	604,000	**2.50**
1909-O	925,000	**2.50**	1914	125,000	**10.00**
1909-S	1¾ million	**2.50**	1914-S	1 million	**2.50**
1910	419,000	**4.00**	1915	138,000	**10.00**
1910-S	2 million	**2.50**	1915-D	1¼ million	**2.50**
1911	1½ million	**2.50**	1915-S	1⅔ million	**2.50**
1911-D	695,000	**2.50**			

Type: Liberty Walking.

(Mint marks: on the coins of 1916 and the early coinage of 1917, the mint marks are on the Obv., under the motto. On the later coinage of 1917 and thereafter, the mint marks are on the Rev., to the left of "Half Dollar.")

Date	Amount Minted	Value	Date	Amount Minted	Value
1916	608,000	**7.00**	1923-S	2¼ million	**4.00**
1916-D	1 million	**6.00**	1927-S	2⅓ million	**2.50**
1916-S	508,000	**15.00**	1928-S	2 million	**3.00**
1917	12¼ million	**3.75**	1929-D	1 million	**3.00**
1917-D (Obv.)	765,000	**5.00**	1929-S	2 million	**2.50**
1917-D (Rev.)	2 million	**3.75**	1933-S	1¾ million	**2.50**
1917-S (Obv.)	1 million	**5.00**	1934	7 million	**2.25**
1917-S (Rev.)	5½ million	**3.75**	1934-D	2⅓ million	**2.25**
1918	6⅔ million	**3.75**	1934-S	3⅔ million	**2.25**
1918-D	3¾ million	**4.00**	1935	9¼ million	**2.25**
1918-S	10¼ million	**3.75**	1935-D	3 million	**2.25**
1919	962,000	**5.00**	1935-S	3¾ million	**2.25**
1919-D	1¼ million	**4.00**	1936	12⅓ million	**2.25**
1919-S	1½ million	**3.75**	1936-D	4¼ million	**2.25**
1920	6⅓ million	**3.75**	1936-S	4 million	**2.25**
1920-D	1½ million	**4.00**	1937	9½ million	**2.25**
1920-S	4⅔ million	**3.75**	1937-D	1¾ million	**2.25**
1921	246,000	**22.50**	1937-S	2 million	**2.25**
1921-D	208,000	**34.00**	1938	4 million	**2.25**
1921-S	548,000	**7.00**	1938-D	491,600	**9.00**

Date	Amount Minted	Value
1939	6¾ million	**2.25**
1939-D	4¼ million	**2.25**
1939-S	2½ million	**2.25**
1940	9¼ million	**2.25**
1940-S	4½ million	**2.25**
1941	24¼ million	**2.25**
1941-D	11¼ million	**2.25**
1941-S	8 million	**2.25**
1942	47¾ million	**2.25**
1942-D	11 million	**2.25**
1942-S	12¾ million	**2.25**
1943	53¼ million	**2.25**
1943-D	11⅓ million	**2.25**
1943-S	13½ million	**2.25**
1944	28¼ million	**2.25**
1944-D	9¾ million	**2.25**
1944-S	9 million	**2.25**
1945	31½ million	**2.25**
1945-D	10 million	**2.25**
1945-S	10¼ million	**2.25**
1946	12 million	**2.25**
1946-D	2¼ million	**2.25**
1946-S	3¾ million	**2.25**
1947	4 million	**2.25**
1947-D	4 million	**2.25**

Type: Franklin Head.

(The mint marks are on the Rev., above the Liberty Bell)

Date	Amount Minted	Value
1948	3 million	**2.50**
1948-D	4 million	**2.50**
1949	5¾ million	**2.50**
1949-D	4 million	**2.50**
1949-S	3¾ million	**3.00**
1950	7¾ million	**2.25**
1950-D	8 million	**2.25**
1951	16¾ million	**2.25**
1951-D	9½ million	**2.25**
1951-S	13⅔ million	**2.25**
1952	21¼ million	**2.25**
1952-D	25⅓ million	**2.25**
1952-S	5½ million	**2.25**
1953	2¾ million	**2.25**
1953-D	21 million	**2.25**
1953-S	4¼ million	**2.25**
1954	13½ million	**2.25**
1954-D	24½ million	**2.25**
1954-S	5 million	**2.25**
1955	3 million	**2.25**
1956	4¼ million	**2.25**
1957	5 million	**2.25**
1957-D	20 million	**2.25**
1958	4 million	**2.25**
1958-D	24 million	**2.25**
1959	6¼ million	**2.25**
1959-D	13 million	**2.25**
1960	7¾ million	**2.25**
1960-D	18¼ million	**2.25**
1961	8¼ million	**2.25**
1961-D	20¼ million	**2.25**
1962	9¾ million	**2.25**
1962-D	35½ million	**2.25**
1963	22 million	**2.25**
1963-D	67 million	**2.25**

Reg. Obv. 1964-1974 | Reg. Rev. 1964-1974 | Bicentennial Obv.—1976 | Bicentennial Rev.—1976

Type: Kennedy Head

(In 1964 the mint mark is on the Rev., under the eagle's right talon. From 1968 to date, the mint marks are on the obverse, just below the base of Kennedy's neck)

Date	*Amount Minted*	*Value*
	SILVER	
1964	277¼ million	**2.25**
1964-D	156¼ million	**2.25**
	SILVER CLAD	
1965	65¾ million	**.70**
1966	109 million	**.70**
1967	295 million	**.70**
1968-D	247 million	**.70**
1968-S	3 million proofs	**2.00**
1969-D	129¾ million	**.70**
1969-S	3 million proofs	**2.00**
1970-D	2¼ million	**10.00**
1970-S	2½ million proofs	**6.00**
	COPPER-NICKEL CLAD	
1971	155¼ million	**.50**
1971-D	302 million	**.50**
1971-S	3¼ million proofs	**.90**
1972	153 million	**.50**
1972-D	141¾ million	**.50**
1972-S	3¼ million proofs	**1.00**
1973	65 million	**.50**
1973-D	83 million	**.50**
1973-S	2¾ million proofs	**1.00**
1974	201½ million	**.50**
1974-D	79 million	**.50**
1974-S	2⅔ million proofs	**1.00**
1975	none minted	
1976-S	234⅓ million	**.50**
1976-D	287½ million	**.50**
1976-S	**cupro-nickel, proof** 7 million	**.75**
1976-S	silver	**1.25**
1976-S	silver, proof	**1.75**
1977	43½ million	**.50**
1977-D	31½ million	**.50**
1977-S	3¼ million proofs	**.85**
1978	14⅓ million	**.50**
1978-D	13¾ million	**.50**
1978-S	3¼ million proofs	**1.00**
1979	68⅓ million	**.50**
1979-D	15¾ million	**.50**
1979-S	3¾ million proofs	**.85**
1980	44 million	**.50**
1980-D	33½ million	**.50**
1980-S proof	3½ million proofs	**.85**
1981	29½ million	**.50**
1981-D	27¾ million	**.50**
1981-S	4 million proofs	**.85**
1982	10.8 million	**.50**
1982-D	13 million	**.50**
1982-S	3.8 million proofs	**2.50**
1983	34 million	**.50**
1983-D	32½ million	**.50**
1983-S	3.8 million proofs	**3.50**
1984	26 million	**.50**
1984-D	26¼ million	**.50**
1984-S	3 million proofs	**2.50**
1985	18.7 million	**.50**
1985-D	19.8 million	**.50**
1985-S	3.4 million proofs	**3.00**
1986	13.1 million	**.50**
1986-D	15.3 million	**.50**
1986-S	3 million proofs	**2.00**
1987		**.50**
1987-D		**.50**
1987-S	proofs	**3.00**
1988		**.50**
1988-D		**.50**
1988-S	proofs	**2.50**

SILVER DOLLARS

Type: Head of Liberty with flowing hair.

Date	Amount Minted	Value	Date	Amount Minted	Value
1794	1,758	**3,250.00**	1795	Part of 184,000	**500.00**

Type: Draped bust of Liberty; with small eagle on Rev.

Date	Amount Minted	Value	Date	Amount Minted	Value
1795	Part of 184,000	**350.00**	1797	7,800	**350.00**
1796	72,900	**350.00**	1798	Part of 327,500	**400.00**

Type: Draped bust of Liberty; with large eagle on Rev.

Date	*Amount Minted*	*Value*
1798	Part of 327,500	**200.00**
1799	423,500	**200.00**
1800	220,900	**200.00**
1801	54,500	**200.00**
1802	41,600	**200.00**
1803	66,100	**200.00**
1804	—	—

(less than 15 specimens are known of the 1804 Dollar.)

Type: Liberty seated; with flying eagle on Rev.—the Gobrecht design.

Date	Amount Minted	Value
1836	About 1,000	**1,000.00**
1838	About 100	**2,000.00**
1839	About 300	**1,300.00**

Type: Liberty seated; without motto over the eagle.

(The mint marks are on the Rev., under the eagle)

Date	Amount Minted	Value	Date	Amount Minted	Value
1840	61,000	**42.00**	1854	33,100	**75.00**
1841	173,000	**40.00**	1855	26,000	**120.00**
1842	184,600	**40.00**	1856	63,500	**70.00**
1843	165,100	**40.00**	1857	94,000	**70.00**
1844	20,000	**75.00**	1858	Proof, About 100	**3,000.00**
1845	24,500	**75.00**	1859	256,500	**40.00**
1846	110,600	**40.00**	1859-O	360,000	**40.00**
1846-O	59,000	**70.00**	1859-S	20,000	**50.00**
1847	140,700	**40.00**	1860	218,900	**40.00**
1848	15,000	**50.00**	1860-O	515,000	**40.00**
1849	62,600	**40.00**	1861	78,500	**70.00**
1850	7,500	**90.00**	1862	12,100	**125.00**
1850-O	40,000	**40.00**	1863	27,700	**75.00**
1851	1,300	**600.00**	1864	31,200	**75.00**
1852	1,100	**Rare**	1865	47,000	**75.00**
1853	46,100	**45.00**			

Type: Liberty seated: with motto over the eagle.

(The mint marks are on the Rev., under the eagle)

Date	Amount Minted	Value	Date	Amount Minted	Value
1866	49,600	**50.00**	1871	1 million	40.00
1867	60,300	**50.00**	1871-CC	1,400	**350.00**
1868	182,700	**45.00**	1872	1 million	40.00
1869	424,300	**40.00**	1872-S	9,000	50.00
1870	433,000	**40.00**	1872-CC	3,100	175.00
1870-S	Unknown	**Rare**	1873	293,600	40.00
1870-CC	12,500	**90.00**	1873-CC	2,300	**450.00**

Type: Liberty Head.

(The mint marks are on the Rev., under the eagle)

Date	Amount Minted	Very Fine	Unc	Date	Amount Minted	Very Fine	Unc
1878	10½ million	**9.00**	**30.00**	1885-O	9¼ million	**8.00**	**22.00**
1878-S	9¾ million	**9.00**	**30.00**	1885-S	1½ million	**9.00**	**50.00**
1878-CC	2¼ million	**11.00**	**65.00**	1885-CC	228,000	**90.00**	**150.00**
1879	14¾ million	**8.00**	**25.00**	1886	20 million	**8.00**	**22.00**
1879-O	3 million	**8.00**	**25.00**	1886-O	10¾ million	**8.00**	**200.00**
1879-S	9 million	**9.00**	**28.00**	1886-S	750,000	**9.00**	**75.00**
1879-CC	756,000	**18.00**	**750.00**	1887	20¼ million	**8.00**	**22.00**
1880	12⅔ million	**8.00**	**25.00**	1887-O	11½ million	**8.00**	**25.00**
1880-O	5⅓ million	**8.00**	**25.00**	1887-S	1¾ million	**9.00**	**25.00**
1880-S	9 million	**9.00**	**27.00**	1888	19¼ million	**8.00**	**22.00**
1880-CC	591,000	**20.00**	**110.00**	1888-O	12¼ million	**8.00**	**25.00**
1881	9¼ million	**8.00**	**24.00**	1888-S	657,000	**11.50**	**90.00**
1881-O	5¾ million	**8.00**	**22.00**	1889	21¾ million	**8.00**	**22.00**
1881-S	12¾ million	**9.00**	**26.00**	1889-O	11¾ million	**8.00**	**45.00**
1881-CC	296,000	**35.00**	**120.00**	1889-S	700,000	**11.00**	**65.00**
1882	11million	**8.00**	**22.00**	1889-CC	350,000	**100.00**	**3,750.00**
1882-O	6 million	**8.00**	**22.00**	1890	16¾ million	**8.00**	**25.00**
1882-S	9¼ million	**9.00**	**31.00**	1890-O	10¾ million	**8.00**	**28.00**
1882-CC	1¼ million	**15.00**	**60.00**	1890-S	8¼ million	**8.00**	**40.00**
1883	12¼ million	**8.00**	**22.00**	1890-CC	2⅓ million	**12.00**	**125.00**
1883-O	8¾ million	**8.00**	**22.00**	1891	8¾ million	**8.00**	**25.00**
1883-S	6¼ million	**9.00**	**200.00**	1891-O	8 million	**8.00**	**30.00**
1883-CC	1¼ million	**15.00**	**60.00**	1891-S	5¼ million	**8.00**	**25.00**
1884	14 million	**8.00**	**24.00**	1891-CC	1⅔ million	**15.00**	**100.00**
1884-O	9¾ million	**8.00**	**22.00**	1892	1 million	**8.00**	**65.00**
1884-S	3¼ million	**10.00**	**1,100.00**	1892-O	2¾ million	**8.00**	**65.00**
1884-CC	1¼ million	**15.00**	**60.00**	1892-S	1¼ million	**9.00**	**4,250.00**
1885	17¾ million	**8.00**	**22.00**	1892-CC	1⅓ million	**15.00**	**200.00**

Date	Amount Minted	Very Fine	Unc
1893	379,000	**25.00**	**175.00**
1893-O	300,000	**35.00**	**700.00**
1893-S	100,000	**800.00**	**13,000.00**
1893-CC	677,000	**60.00**	**700.00**
1894	111,000	**125.00**	**700.00**
1894-O	1¾ million	**10.00**	**300.00**
1894-S	1¼ million	**17.00**	**200.00**
1895	880 proofs		**10,000.00**
1895-O	450,000	**40.00**	**1,200.00**
1895-S	400,000	**70.00**	**500.00**
1896	10 million	**8.00**	**14.00**
1896-O	5 million	**11.00**	**450.00**
1896-S	5 million	**18.00**	**200.00**
1897	2¾ million	**8.00**	**14.00**
1897-O	4 million	**8.00**	**240.00**
1897-S	5¾ million	**11.00**	**20.00**
1898	5¾ million	**8.00**	**14.00**
1898-O	4½ million	**8.00**	**14.00**
1898-S	4 million	**8.00**	**75.00**
1899	331,000	**15.00**	**50.00**

Date	Amount Minted	Very Fine	Unc
1899-O	12¼ million	**8.00**	**14.00**
1899-S	2½ million	**11.00**	**70.00**
1900	8¾ million	**8.00**	**14.00**
1900-O	12½ million	**8.00**	**14.00**
1900-S	3½ million	**11.00**	**70.00**
1901	7 million	**13.00**	**650.00**
1901-O	13⅓ million	**8.00**	**14.00**
1901-S	2¼ million	**12.00**	**150.00**
1902	8 million	**11.00**	**20.00**
1902-O	8⅔ million	**8.00**	**14.00**
1902-S	1½ million	**25.00**	**100.00**
1903	4⅔ million	**8.00**	**20.00**
1903-O	4½ million	**90.00**	**150.00**
1903-S	1¼ million	**25.00**	**1,000.00**
1904	2¾ million	**8.00**	**45.00**
1904-O	3¾ million	**8.00**	**14.00**
1904-S	2⅓ million	**20.00**	**500.00**
1921	44⅔ million	**7.00**	**10.00**
1921-D	20⅓ million	**7.00**	**14.00**
1921-S	21⅔ million	**7.00**	**14.00**

Type: The Peace Dollar

(The mint marks are on the bottom of the Rev., to left of the eagle's wing)

Date	Amount Minted	Very Fine	Unc
1921	1 million	**14.00**	**100.00**
1922	51¾ million	**7.00**	**10.00**
1922-D	15 million	**7.00**	**22.00**
1922-S	17½ million	**7.00**	**22.00**
1923	30¾ million	**7.00**	**10.00**
1923-D	6¾ million	**7.00**	**22.00**
1923-S	19 million	**7.00**	**15.00**
1924	11¾ million	**8.00**	**13.00**
1924-S	1¾ million	**9.00**	**55.00**
1925	10¼ million	**8.00**	**13.00**
1925-S	1⅔ million	**8.00**	**50.00**
1926	2 million	**8.00**	**15.00**

Date	Amount Minted	Very Fine	Unc
1926-D	2⅓ million	**9.00**	**30.00**
1926-S	7 million	**8.00**	**15.00**
1927	848,000	**9.00**	**35.00**
1927-D	1¼ million	**9.00**	**100.00**
1927-S	866,000	**9.00**	**65.00**
1928	361,000	**55.00**	**135.00**
1928-S	1⅔ million	**9.00**	**60.00**
1934	954,000	**9.00**	**45.00**
1934-D	1½ million	**9.00**	**55.00**
1934-S	1 million	**20.00**	**750.00**
1935	1½ million	**8.00**	**30.00**
1935-S	2 million	**8.00**	**65.00**

Reg. Obv.
1971-1974

Reg. Rev.
1971-1974

Bicentennial
Obv.—1976

Bicentennial
Rev.—1976

Type: The Eisenhower Dollar

(The mint marks are on the obverse, below Eisenhower's neck)
(The valuations are for uncirculated coins)

Date	*Amount Minted*	*Value*
1971 cupro-nickel,	47¾ million	**1.25**
1971-Dcupro-nickel,	68½ million	**1.25**
1971-Ssilver,	6¾ million	**2.50**
1971-Ssilver, proof,	4¼ million	**3.00**
1972 cupro-nickel,	75¾ million	**1.25**
1972-Dcupro-nickel,	92½ million	**1.25**
1972-Ssilver,	2¼ million	**4.00**
1972-Ssilver, proof,	2 million	**5.00**
1973 cupro-nickel,	2 million	**2.50**
1973-D cupro-nickel,	2 million	**2.50**
1973-S cupro-nickel, proof,	2¾ million	**2.50**
1973-Ssilver,	1¾ million	**7.00**
1973-Ssilver, proof,	1 million	**25.00**
1974 cupro-nickel,	27⅓ million	**1.00**
1974-Dcupro-nickel,	45½ million	**1.00**
1974-Sc.n., proof,	2⅔ million	**2.50**
1974-Ssilver,	2 million	**6.00**
1974-Ssilver, proof,	1⅓ million	**7.50**
1975	none minted	
1976		**1.00**
1976-D		**1.00**
1976-S cupro-nickel, proof		**2.00**
1976-S silver		**3.50**
1976-Ssilver, proof		**6.00**
1977 cupro-nickel,	12½ million	**1.00**
1977-Dcupro-nickel,	33 million	**1.00**
1977-Sc.n., proof,	3¼ million	**2.00**
1978 cupro-nickel,	25¾ million	**1.00**
1978-D cupro-nickel,	23 million	**1.00**
1978-S c.n, proof,	3 million	**2.25**

Type: The Anthony Dollar

(The mint marks are on the Obv., to the left of Anthony's neck. The valuations are for Uncirculated coins)

Type I—Mint mark is not distinct. Type II—Mint mark is clear.

Date	*Amount Minted*	*Value*
1979-P	360¼ million	**1.00**
1979-D	288 million	**1.00**
1979-S	109½ million	**1.10**
1979-S Ty. I	3½ million proofs	**4.00**
1979-S Ty. II	proof	**45.00**
1980-P	27½ million	**1.00**
1980-D	41½ million	**1.00**
1980-S	20½ million	**1.10**
1980-S	3½ million proofs	**4.00**
1981-P	3 million	**2.00**
1981-D	3¼ million	**2.00**
1981-S	3½ million	**2.00**
1981-S Ty. I	4 million proofs	**3.25**
1981-S Ty. II	proof	**40.00**

Type: The Trade Dollar

(The mint marks are on the Rev., under the eagle)

Date	*Amount Minted*	*Value*
1873	397,500	**30.00**
1873-S	703,000	**30.00**
1873-CC	124,500	**35.00**
1874	987,800	**30.00**
1874-S	2½ million	**30.00**
1874-CC	1⅓ million	**30.00**
1875	218,900	**40.00**
1875-S	4½ million	**30.00**
1875-CC	1½ million	**30.00**
1876	456,100	**30.00**
1876-S	5¼ million	**30.00**
1876-CC	509,000	**35.00**
1877	3 million	**30.00**
1877-S	9½ million	**30.00**
1877-CC	534,000	**35.00**
1878	900 Proofs	**2,000.00**
1878-S	4¼ million	**30.00**
1878-CC	97,000	**70.00**
1879	1,500 Proofs	**2,000.00**
1880	2,000 Proofs	**2,000.00**
1881	1,000 Proofs	**2,000.00**
1882	1,100 Proofs	**2,000.00**
1883	1,000 Proofs	**2,000.00**
1884	10 Proofs	——
1885	5 Proofs	——

U.S. Silver Commemorative Coins

(All are Half Dollars of standard size and weight except the Isabella Quarter of 1893, the Lafayette Dollar of 1900, the Olympic coins of 1984, the Immigrant Half Dollar of 1986, and the Ellis Island Dollar.)

IMPORTANT NOTE: **The valuations below are for coins in bright, new, uncirculated condition.** Pieces in used or circulated condition are worth less. The amount of coins minted or in existence is shown to the left of the valuation. Because of speculation, the valuations are subject to fluctuation. Coins in exceptionally choice condition are worth considerably more than the prices listed.

COLUMBIAN, 1892-1893

For the World's Columbian Exposition of Chicago, where it was issued on the 400th year of the discovery of America. Head of Columbus. Rev. His flagship, the Santa Maria, over global hemispheres.

1892	950,000 (used **4.50**)	**35.00**
1893	1½ million (used **4.50**)	**35.00**

ISABELLA QUARTER, 1893

For the same event as the Columbian Half Dollar. Crowned head of Queen Isabella of Spain. Rev. Female spinner kneeling.

1893	24,191	**300.00**

LAFAYETTE DOLLAR, 1900

On the gift by the youth of America to France of an equestrian statue of Lafayette. Conjoined heads of Washington and Lafayette. Rev. The statue as erected in Paris.

1900	36,026	**500.00**

PANAMA-PACIFIC, 1915

For the Panama-Pacific Exposition in San Francisco on the opening of the Panama Canal. Columbia and child standing at the Golden Gate. Rev. Eagle and shield.

1915-S	27,134	**250.00**

ILLINOIS, 1981

On the 100th year of Illinois statehood. Head of Lincoln. Rev. Eagle standing to left.

1918	100,058	**75.00**

MAINE, 1920

On the 100th year of Maine statehood. The coat-of-arms of Maine. Rev. Wreath formed of pines and cones.

1920	50,028	**70.00**

PILGRIM, 1920-1921

On the 300th year of the Landing of the Pilgrims at Plymouth Rock. Governor Bradford in Pilgrim dress. Rev. The ship Mayflower.

1920	152,000	**30.00**
1921	20,053	**85.00**

MISSOURI, 1921

On the 100th year of Missouri statehood. Bust of a Missouri pioneer. Rev. Pioneer and Indian standing. The "2 × 4" is located in front of the bust.

1921	15,400	**300.00**
1921 2 × 4	5,000	**325.00**

ALABAMA, 1921

On the 100th year of Alabama statehood. Conjoined heads of Gov. Bibb (1821) and Gov. Kilby (1921). Rev. Eagle. The "2 × 2" is located in the back of the busts.

1921	49,000	**150.00**
1921 2 × 2	5,000	**210.00**

GRANT, 1922

On the 100th year of his birth. Uniformed bust of the General. Rev. A log cabin in the woods. The * is located on the obverse, over the word, "Grant." Beware of added star.

1922	67,200	**70.00**
1922*	4,250	**475.00**

MONROE DOCTRINE, 1923

On the 100th year of Monroe's famous Doctrine. Conjoined heads of Monroe and John Q. Adams. Rev. Allegories depicting North and South America.

1923-S	274,077	**40.00**

HUGUENOT-WALLOON, 1924

On the 300th year of the settlement of New Netherlands by the Dutch. Conjoined heads of Admiral Coligny and William the Silent. Rev. The ship New Netherlands.

1924	142,080	**75.00**

LEXINGTON-CONCORD, 1925

On the 150th year of these famous battles of 1775. Armed Minute Man standing. Rev. View of Old Belfry.

1925	162,099	**35.00**

STONE MOUNTAIN, 1925

On the erection of a Memorial on Stone Mountain to the valor of the Soldier of the South. Gen. "Stonewall" Jackson and Gen. Robert E. Lee on horseback. Rev. Eagle on mountain peak.

1925	1⅓ million (used **9.00**)	**27.00**

CALIFORNIA JUBILEE, 1925

On the 75th year of California Statehood. A "forty-niner" panning gold. Rev. Grizzly bear.

1925-S	86,500	**95.00**

FORT VANCOUVER, 1925

On the 100th year of the erection of Fort Vancouver. Head of Dr. John McLoughlin, who built the Fort. Rev. Armed pioneer standing before mountain.

1925	14,994	**275.00**

U.S. INDEPENDENCE, 1926

On the 150th year of the Declaration of Independence. Conjoined heads of Washington and Coolidge. Rev. The Liberty Bell.

1926	141,120	**40.00**

OREGON TRAIL, 1926-1939

In commemoration of this popular but perilous highway to the west. Indian Chief standing before a map of the U.S. Rev. The famous covered wagon of the Trail.

1926	48,030	**75.00**
1926-S	86,354	**75.00**
1928	6,028	**150.00**
1933-D	5,008	**175.00**
1934-D	7,006	**135.00**
1936	10,006	**100.00**
1936-S	5,006	**150.00**
1937-D	12,008	**90.00**
1938-P-D-S	6,005 sets, set of 3	**400.00**
1939-P-D-S	3,004 sets, set of 3	**800.00**

VERMONT, 1927

On the 150th year both of the Battle of Bennington and of Vermont's independence. Head of Ira Allen. Rev. Vermont mountain lion.

1927	28,142	**160.00**

HAWAII, 1928

On the 150th year of Captain Cook's discovery of the Hawaiian Islands. Bust of the Captain. Rev. Hawaiian Chief in native dress.

1928	10,008	**550.00**

MARYLAND, 1934

On the 300th year of the founding of the Colony. Head of Lord Baltimore, the founder. Rev. The coat-of-arms of Maryland.

1934	25,015	**95.00**

BOONE, 1934–1938

On the 200th year of the birth of Daniel Boone. Head of Boone. Rev. Standing figures of Boone and Indian Chief, Black Fish.

1934	10,007		**85.00**
1935	10,010	Set of	
1935-D-S	5,005 per mint	3	**700.00**

The following have the date "1934" on the reverse about "Pioneer Year."

1935	10,008	Set of	
1935-P-D-S	2,003 per Mint	3	**275.00**
1936	12,012	Set of	
1936-P-D-S	5,006 per Mint	3	**275.00**
1937	9,810	Set of	
1937-P-D-S	2,506 per Mint	3	**500.00**
1938-P-D-S	2,100	Set of 3	**750.00**
Type coin (any date)			**70.00**

TEXAS, 1934-1938

On the 100th year of the Independence of Texas. Eagle on a "lone star." Rev. Winged Victory between heads of Sam Houston and Stephen Austin.

1934	61,350	**85.00**
1935	9,934	**90.00**
1935-D	10,007	**90.00**
1935-S	10,008	**90.00**
1936	8,911	**90.00**
1936-D	9,039	**90.00**
1936-S	9,064	**90.00**
1937-P-D-S	6,571 sets, set of 3	**275.00**
1938-P-D-S	3,775 sets, set of 3	**500.00**

ARKANSAS, 1935-1939

On the 100th year of Arkansas Statehood. Liberty head and Indian head conjoined. Rev. Eagle.

1935	13,012	**60.00**
1935-D-S	5,505 pair, set of 2	**120.00**
1936-P-D-S	9,660 sets, set of 3	**180.00**
1937-P-D-S	5,505 sets, set of 3	**190.00**
1938-P-D-S	3,155 sets, set of 3	**350.00**
1939-P-D-S	2,104 sets, set of 3	**700.00**

CONNECTICUT, 1935

On the 300th year of the founding of the Colony. The famous Charter Oak Tree. Rev. Eagle.

1935	25,018	**175.00**

HUDSON, 1935

On the 150th year of the founding of the city of Hudson, N.Y. Hudson's ship, the Half Moon. Rev. Neptune on whale, a mermaid in the background.

1935	10,008	**375.00**

SAN DIEGO, 1935-1936

For the California-Pacific International Exposition in San Diego. Seated female and bear. View of Exposition buildings.

1935-S	70,132	**65.00**
1936-D	30,092	**70.00**

OLD SPANISH TRAIL, 1935

On the 400th year of the de Vaca Expedition across the land area of the Gulf of Mexico. Skull of a cow. Rev. Yucca tree and map of the Trail.

1935	10,008	**500.00**

ALBANY, 1936

On the 250th year of Albany's City Charter. Beaver gnawing on maple twigs. Rev. Standing figures of Gov. Dongan, Peter Schuyler and Robert Livingston.

1936	16,887	**225.00**

BRIDGEPORT, 1936

On the 100th year of Bridgeport, Conn. as a city. Head of P. T. Barnum. Rev. Modern style eagle.

1936	25,015	**120.00**

CINCINNATI, 1936

On the 50th year of Cincinnati as a music center. Head of Stephen Foster. Rev. Girl playing harp.

1936	5,005	**225.00**
1936-D	5,005	**225.00**
1936-S	5,006	**225.00**

COLUMBIA, S.C., 1936

On the 150th year of the founding of the city. Standing figure of Justice between the Capitol buildings of 1786 and 1936. Rev. Palmetto tree.

1936	9.007	**225.00**
1936-D	8,009	**225.00**
1936-S	8,007	**225.00**

DELAWARE, 1936

On the 300th year of the Swedish landing in Wilmington. The Swedish ship Kalmar Nyckel. Rev. Old Swede's Church in Wilmington.

1936	25,015	**175.00**

ELGIN, ILLINOIS, 1936

On the 100th year of the founding of the city. Bearded head of a pioneer. Rev. Four pioneers standing.

1936	25,015	**200.00**

GETTYSBURG, 1936

For the 75th Anniversary of the Battle of Gettysburg, 1863-1938. Conjoined heads of a Union and Confederate soldier. Rev. Union and Confederate shields.

1936	26,928	**175.00**

GREAT LAKES, 1936

For the Great Lakes Exposition on the 100th year of Cleveland, Ohio. Head of Moses Cleaveland. Rev. Map of the Great Lakes.

1936	50,030	**60.00**

LONG ISLAND, 1936

On the 300th year of the landing at Jamaica Bay, Long Island by Dutch Settlers. Conjoined heads of a Dutchman and Indian. Rev. Sailing ship.

1936	81,773	**55.00**

LYNCHBURG, 1936

On the 150th year of the city charter given to Lynchburg, Virginia. Head of Senator Carter Glass. Rev. Liberty standing at old courthouse.

1936	20,013	**125.00**

NORFOLK, 1936

On the 200th year of Norfolk, Virginia, becoming a royal borough. Sailing ship as on the city shield. Rev. A large mace.

1936	15,000	**400.00**

RHODE ISLAND, 1936

On the 300th year of the founding of Providence by Roger Williams. Roger Williams in canoe being welcomed by Indian. Rev. Large anchor.

1936	20,013	**65.00**
1936-D	15,010	**65.00**
1936-S	15,011	**65.00**

ROBINSON, 1936

On the 100th year of Arkansas statehood. Head of Senator Joseph T. Robinson. Rev. Eagle. (Identical to the reverse of the Arkansas issues of 1935-1939; the only instance of the same event being commemorated by two different types of Half Dollars.)

1936	25,265	**70.00**

SAN FRANCISCO, 1936

On the opening of the San Francisco-Oakland Bay Bridge. California grizzly bear. Rev. View of the bridge.

1936-S	71,369	**125.00**

WISCONSIN, 1936

On the 100th year of the formation of Wisconsin Territory. Forearm holding pickaxe over ore. Rev. Badger on log.

1936	25,015	**160.00**

YORK COUNTY, ME., 1936

On the 300th year of the founding of York County, Maine. Brown's Garrison at Saco. Rev. The seal of the County.

1936	25,015	**175.00**

ANTIETAM, 1937

On the 75th year of the Battle of Antietam. Conjoined heads of the Union's Gen. McClellan and the Confederacy's Gen. Lee. Rev. Burnside Bridge for which the battle was fought.

1937	18,028	**300.00**

ROANOKE, 1937

On the 350th year of the colonization of Roanoke Island by Sir Walter Raleigh; also on the birth of Virginia Dare in 1587, the first white child born in America. Bust of Sir Walter Raleigh. Rev. Mother holding Virginia Dare.

1937	29,030	**165.00**

NEW ROCHELLE, 1938

On the 250th year of the founding of New Rochelle, New York, by the Huguenots. Lord Pell holding fatted calf. Rev. Fleur-de-lis.

1938	15,266	**275.00**

IOWA, 1946

On the 100th year of Iowa Statehood. Eagle on scroll. Rev. The old Capitol Statehouse at Iowa City.

1946	100,057	**60.00**

B.T.W., 1946-1951

In honor of this great black leader and educator. Head of Booker T. Washington. Rev. View of the log cabin of his birth and of the Hall of Fame where he is inscribed.

1946	1 million	**6.00**
1946-D	200,113	**8.00**
1946-S	500,279	**7.00**
1947-P-D-S	100,017 sets, set of 3	**35.00**
1948-P-D-S	8,005 sets, set of 3	**60.00**
1949-P-D-S	6,004 sets, set of 3	**65.00**
1950-P-D-S	6,004 sets, set of 3	**65.00**
1950-S	403,996	**8.00**
1951	503,078	**8.00**
1951-P-D-S	7,004 sets, set of 3	**50.00**

G.W.C.-B.T.W., 1951-1954

In honor of the famous black leaders, George Washington Carver and Booker T. Washington. Their conjoined heads. Rev. Map of the United States.

1951	100,014	**7.00**
1951-P-D-S	10,004 sets, set of 3	**50.00**
1952	2 million	**7.00**
1952-P-D-S	8,000 sets, set of 3	**50.00**
1953-P-D-S	8,000 sets, set of 3	**60.00**
1953-S	100,000	**9.00**
1954-P-D-S	12,000 sets, set of 3	**50.00**
1954-S	110,000	**9.00**

GEORGE WASHINGTON, 1982

On the 250th Anniversary of the birth of the first President. Washington on horseback. Rev. View of Mount Vernon.

1982-D	Uncirculated	**6.00**
1982-S	Proof	**6.00**

LOS ANGELES OLYMPIC GAMES, 1983–1984

Issued to help raise funds for the staging of the 1984 Summer Olympic Games in Los Angeles. Both issues bear an eagle on the obverse, with the reverse of the 1983 coin depicting a discus thrower and the 1984 coin the gateway to the Los Angeles Coliseum.

1 Dollar	1983-P Unc.	920,485	**16.00**
1 Dollar	1983-D Unc.	597,157	**30.00**
1 Dollar	1983-S Unc.	662,837	**20.00**
1 Dollar	1983-S Proof	4,575,603	**16.00**
1 Dollar	1984-P Unc.	470,131	**15.00**
1 Dollar	1984-D Unc.	316,778	**60.00**
1 Dollar	1984-S Unc.	339,970	**40.00**
1 Dollar	1984-S Proof	2,623,609	**16.00**

IMMIGRANT, 1986

On the centennial of the Statue of Liberty. Commemorates the immigrants who passed through Ellis Island before entering New York. Rising sun behind statue. Rev. Immigrant Family on Ellis Island.

1986-D	Uncirculated	**4.00**
1986-S	Proof	**5.00**

ELLIS ISLAND, 1986

On the centennial of the Statue of Liberty. Commemorates Ellis Island, the "Gateway to America." Statue in front of the Ellis Island immigration facility. Rev. Liberty's hand holding torch.

1986-P	Uncirculated	**15.00**
1986-S	Proof	**16.00**

Coins shown at approximately 4/5 actual size.

CONSTITUTION BICENTENNIAL, 1987

On the 200th anniversary of the Constitution of the United States. Quill pen superimposed over a copy of the Constitution. Rev. A group of American men and women from the past two centuries.

1987-P	Uncirculated	**12.50**
1987-S	Proof	**12.00**

Coins shown at approximately 85% of actual size.

1988 OLYMPICS

To raise money for the 1988 American Olympic Teams. Two torches. Rev. Rings.

1988-D	Uncirculated	**17.50**
1988-S	Proof	**20.00**

U.S. Gold Commemorative Coins

IMPORTANT NOTE: The valuations below are for coins in bright, new, uncirculated condition. Pieces in used or circulated condition are worth less. The amount of coins minted or in existence is shown to the left of the valuation.

LOUISIANA PURCHASE ISSUE, 1903

Two types of Gold Dollars were struck to commemorate the Centennial of the Louisiana Purchase. The same reverse appears on both.

1 Dollar 1903	Head of Jefferson	17,375	**500.00**
1 Dollar 1903	Head of McKinley	17,375	**500.00**

LEWIS AND CLARK ISSUE, 1904–1905

Two dates of a Gold Dollar were struck to commemorate the Centennial of the Lewis and Clark Expedition. The head of Lewis appears on one side and that of Clark on the other.

1 Dollar 1904	9,997	**800.00**
1 Dollar 1905	10,000	**800.00**

PANAMA PACIFIC ISSUE, 1915

Four types of gold coins were struck for the Panama-Pacific Exposition commemorating the opening of the Panama Canal.

1 Dollar 1915-S	Head of worker	25,000	**500.00**

2½ Dollars 1915-S	Columbia on hippocampus	6,749	**1,200.00**

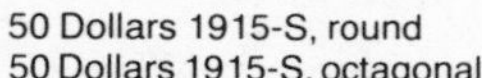

50 Dollars 1915-S, round	Head of Minerva	483	**17,000.00**
50 Dollars 1915-S, octagonal	Head of Minerva	645	**15,000.00**

McKINLEY MEMORIAL ISSUE, 1916–1917

Two dates of a Gold Dollar were struck to commemorate the erection of the McKinley Memorial at Niles, Ohio. The obverse shows his head, and the reverse the memorial building.

1 Dollar 1916	9,977	**500.00**
1 Dollar 1917	10,000	**525.00**

GRANT CENTENNIAL ISSUE, 1922

Two varieties of a Gold Dollar were struck to commemorate the 100th year of Grant's birth. His head appears on the obverse and a log cabin on the reverse. The star is located on the obverse, over the word, "Grant."

1 Dollar 1922	5,000	**1,200.00**
1 Dollar 1922 with star	5,000	**1,200.00**

U.S. INDEPENDENCE ISSUE, 1926

A 2½ Dollar gold piece was struck to commemorate the Sesquicentennial (150th year) of the Declaration of Independence. The obverse shows Liberty standing; the reverse a view of Independence Hall in Philadelphia.

2½ Dollars 1926	46,019	**400.00**

LOS ANGELES OLYMPIC GAMES, 1984

To raise funds for the staging of the Games. Struck at the West Point, NY Mint facility.

10 Dollars	1984-W Unc.	100,000	**225.00**
10 Dollars	1984-W Proof	661,000	**200.00**
10 Dollars	1984-P Proof only	40,000	**500.00**
10 Dollars	1984-D Proof only	44,000	**300.00**
10 Dollars	1984-S Proof only	55,000	**250.00**

STATUE OF LIBERTY, 1986

On the centennial of the Statue of Liberty. Head of statue. Rev. American eagle in flight.

5 Dollars	1986-W	Uncirculated	500,000	**200.00**
5 Dollars	1986-W	Proof	500,000	**150.00**

CONSTITUTION BICENTENNIAL, 1987

Coins shown at approximately 150% of actual size.

On the 200th anniversary of the U.S. Constitution. Eagle holding quill pen. Rev. Quill pen under "We the People."

5 Dollars	1987-W	Uncirculated	**100.00**
5 Dollars	1987-W	Proof	**100.00**

1988 OLYMPICS

To raise money for the 1988 American Olympic Teams. Head of Liberty. Rev. Flame.

5 Dollars	1988-W	Uncirculated	**150.00**
5 Dollars	1988-W	Proof	**175.00**

(The valuations in this book are based on the coins being in G-VG condition, unless otherwise noted.)

United States Gold Coins

(The valuations are for coins in choice VF-EF condition. Americans traveling abroad are cautioned to beware of counterfeit U.S. gold pieces in all denominations, which have been produced in many parts of Europe and Asia.)

1 DOLLAR GOLD PIECES

Type: Liberty head with coronet. Small size.

(The mint marks are on the Rev., under the wreath)

Date	*Amount minted*	*Value*	*Date*	*Amount minted*	*Value*
1849	688,600	**110.00**	1852	2 million	**110.00**
1849-O	215,000	**110.00**	1852-O	140,000	**110.00**
1849-C	11,600	**250.00**	1852-C	9,400	**200.00**
1849-D	21,600	**200.00**	1852-D	6,400	**225.00**
1850	482,000	**110.00**	1853	4 million	**110.00**
1850-O	14,000	**110.00**	1853-O	290,000	**110.00**
1850-C	7,000	**250.00**	1853-C	11,500	**250.00**
1850-D	8,400	**200.00**	1853-D	6,600	**250.00**
1851	3⅓ million	**110.00**	1854	Part of 1⅔ million	**110.00**
1851-O	290,000	**110.00**	1854-D	2,900	**375.00**
1851-C	41,300	**200.00**	1854-S	14,600	**110.00**
1851-D	9,900	**225.00**			

Type: Small Liberty head with feather head-dress. Large size.

(The mint marks are on the Rev., under the wreath)

Date	*Amount Minted*	*Value*	*Date*	*Amount Minted*	*Value*
1854	Part of 1⅔ million	**200.00**	1855-C	9,800	**600.00**
1855	758,300	**200.00**	1855-D	1,800	**2,000.00**
1855-O	55,000	**225.00**	1856-S	24,600	**225.00**

Type: Large Liberty head with feather head-dress. Large size.

(The mint marks are on the Rev., under the wreath)

Date	*Amount Minted*	*Value*	*Date*	*Amount Minted*	*Value*
1856	1¾ million	**100.00**	1868	10,500	**125.00**
1856-D	1,500	**2,000.00**	1869	5,900	**125.00**
1857	774,800	**100.00**	1870	6,300	**125.00**
1857-C	13,300	**125.00**	1870-S	3,000	**475.00**
1857-D	3,500	**350.00**	1871	3,900	**125.00**
1857-S	10,000	**150.00**	1872	3,500	**125.00**
1858	118,000	**100.00**	1873	125,100	**100.00**
1858-D	3,500	**600.00**	1874	198,800	**100.00**
1858-S	10,000	**125.00**	1875	400	**1,500.00**
1859	168,200	**100.00**	1876	3,200	**125.00**
1859-C	5,200	**400.00**	1877	3,900	**125.00**
1859-D	5,000	**400.00**	1878	3,000	**125.00**
1859-S	15,000	**125.00**	1879	3,000	**125.00**
1860	36,700	**100.00**	1880	1,600	**125.00**
1860-D	1,600	**1,400.00**	1881	7,700	**100.00**
1860-S	13,000	**125.00**	1882	5,000	**100.00**
1861	527,500	**100.00**	1883	10,800	**100.00**
1861-D	Unknown	**2,000.00**	1884	6,200	**100.00**
1862	1⅓ million	**100.00**	1885	12,200	**100.00**
1863	6,200	**225.00**	1886	6,000	**100.00**
1864	5,900	**200.00**	1887	8,500	**100.00**
1865	3,700	**200.00**	1888	16,100	**100.00**
1866	7,200	**125.00**	1889	30,700	**100.00**
1867	5,200	**125.00**			

2½ DOLLAR GOLD PIECES (QUARTER EAGLES)

Type: Liberty head; without stars on Obv.

Date	*Amount Minted*	*Value*
1796	Part of 1,400	**7,000.00**

Type: Liberty head; with stars on Obv.

Date	Amount Minted	Value	Date	Amount Minted	Value
1796	Part of 1,400	**4,000.00**	1804	3,300	**1,500.00**
1797	1,700	**3,000.00**	1805	1,800	**1,800.00**
1798	600	**2,000.00**	1806	1,600	**1,800.00**
1802 over 1	2,600	**1,500.00**	1807	6,800	**1,500.00**

Type: Draped bust of Liberty with round cap.

Date	Amount Minted	Value
1808	2,700	**6,000.00**

Type: Undraped head of Liberty with round cap; with motto over eagle.

Date	Amount Minted	Value	Date	Amount Minted	Value
1821	6,400	**2,500.00**	1831	4,500	**2,250.00**
1824 over 21	2,600	**2,500.00**	1832	4,400	**2,250.00**
1825	4,400	**2,500.00**	1833	4,200	**2,250.00**
1826 over 25	800	**3,000.00**	1834	4,000	**3,000.00**
1827	2,800	**2,500.00**			
1829	3,400	**2,250.00**			
1830	4,500	**2,250.00**			

Type: Liberty head with ribbon; without motto over eagle.

(The mint marks are on the Obv., over the date)

Date	Amount Minted	Value	Date	Amount Minted	Value
1834	112,200	**150.00**	1838-C	7,900	**275.00**
1835	131,400	**150.00**	1839	27,000	**150.00**
1836	548,000	**150.00**	1839-O	17,800	**250.00**
1837	45,100	**150.00**	1839-C	18,200	**275.00**
1838	47,000	**150.00**	1839-D	13,700	**300.00**

Type: Liberty head with coronet.

(The mint marks are on the Rev., under the eagle. The "CAL" on the 1848 is over the eagle and represents gold mined in California)

Date	Amount Minted	Value	Date	Amount Minted	Value
1840	18,900	**150.00**	1846-C	4,800	**250.00**
1840-O	26,200	**150.00**	1846-D	19,300	**160.00**
1840-C	12,800	**275.00**	1847	29,800	**150.00**
1840-D	3,500	**500.00**	1847-O	124,000	**150.00**
1841	A few proofs	—	1847-C	23,200	**160.00**
1841-C	10,300	**300.00**	1847-D	15,800	**160.00**
1841-D	4,200	**400.00**	1848	7,500	**300.00**
1842	2,800	**300.00**	1848-CAL	1,400	**3,000.00**
1842-O	19,800	**150.00**	1848-C	16,800	**200.00**
1842-C	6,700	**300.00**	1848-D	13,800	**250.00**
1842-D	4,600	**400.00**	1849	23,300	**120.00**
1843	100,500	**150.00**	1849-C	10,200	**200.00**
1843-O	368,000	**150.00**	1849-D	10,900	**200.00**
1843-C	26,100	**300.00**	1850	252,900	**120.00**
1843-D	36,200	**300.00**	1850-O	84,000	**120.00**
1844	6,800	**150.00**	1850-C	9,100	**200.00**
1844-C	11,600	**160.00**	1850-D	12,100	**200.00**
1844-D	17,300	**160.00**	1851	1⅓ million	**120.00**
1845	91,100	**150.00**	1851-O	148,000	**120.00**
1845-O	4,000	**250.00**	1851-C	14,900	**200.00**
1845-D	19,500	**160.00**	1851-D	11,300	**200.00**
1846	21,600	**150.00**	1852	1¼ million	**120.00**
1846-O	66,000	**150.00**	1852-O	142,000	**120.00**

2½ Dollar Gold Pieces (continued)

Date	Amount Minted	Value
1852-C	9,800	**200.00**
1852-D	4,000	**275.00**
1853	1⅓ million	**120.00**
1853-D	3,200	**275.00**
1854	596,300	**120.00**
1854-O	153,000	**120.00**
1854-C	7,300	**200.00**
1854-D	1,800	**1,000.00**
1854-S	246	**10,000.00**
1855	235,500	**120.00**
1855-C	3,700	**375.00**
1855-D	1,100	**900.00**
1856	384,200	**120.00**
1856-O	21,100	**140.00**
1856-C	7,900	**200.00**
1856-D	874	**1,500.00**
1856-S	71,100	**140.00**
1857	214,100	**120.00**
1857-O	34,000	**120.00**
1857-D	2,400	**250.00**
1857-S	68,000	**120.00**
1858	47,400	**120.00**
1858-C	9,100	**175.00**
1859	39,400	**120.00**
1859-D	2,200	**250.00**
1859-S	15,200	**120.00**
1860	22,700	**120.00**
1860-C	7,500	**175.00**
1860-S	35,600	**120.00**
1861	1¼ million	**120.00**
1861-S	24,000	**140.00**
1862	112,400	**120.00**
1862-S	8,000	**140.00**
1863	30 proofs	—
1863-S	10,800	**120.00**
1864	2,900	**375.00**
1865	1,500	**375.00**
1865-S	23,400	**120.00**
1866	3,100	**175.00**
1866-S	39,000	**120.00**
1867	3,200	**175.00**
1867-S	28,000	**120.00**
1868	3,600	**165.00**
1868-S	34,000	**120.00**
1869	4,300	**150.00**
1869-S	29,500	**120.00**
1870	4,600	**150.00**
1870-S	16,000	**120.00**
1871	5,300	**150.00**
1871-S	22,000	**120.00**
1872	3,000	**165.00**
1872-S	18,000	**120.00**
1873	178,000	**120.00**
1873-S	27,000	**120.00**
1874	3,900	**160.00**
1875	420	**1,000.00**
1875-S	11,600	**120.00**
1876	4,200	**150.00**
1876-S	5,000	**140.00**
1877	1,700	**200.00**
1877-S	35,400	**120.00**
1878	286,300	**120.00**
1878-S	178,000	**120.00**
1879	89,000	**120.00**
1879-S	43,500	**120.00**
1880	3,000	**120.00**
1881	680	**300.00**
1882	4,000	**140.00**
1883	2,000	**165.00**
1884	2,000	**165.00**
1885	887	**300.00**
1886	4,100	**150.00**
1887	6,300	**120.00**
1888	16,100	**120.00**
1889	17,600	**120.00**
1890	8,800	**120.00**
1891	11,000	**120.00**
1892	2,500	**120.00**
1893	30,100	**120.00**
1894	4,100	**140.00**

Date	Amount Minted	Value	Date	Amount Minted	Value
1895	6,100	**140.00**	1902	133,700	**120.00**
1896	19,200	**120.00**	1903	201,300	**120.00**
1897	29,900	**120.00**	1904	161,000	**120.00**
1898	24,200	**120.00**	1905	217,900	**120.00**
1899	27,300	**120.00**	1906	176,500	**120.00**
1900	67,200	**120.00**	1907	336,400	**120.00**
1901	91,300	**120.00**			

Type: Indian Head

(The mint marks are on the Rev., to the left of the value)

Date	Amount Minted	Value	Date	Amount Minted	Value
1908	565,000	**120.00**	1914-D	448,000	**120.00**
1909	441,900	**120.00**	1915	606,100	**120.00**
1910	492,700	**120.00**	1925-D	578,000	**120.00**
1911	704,200	**120.00**	1926	446,000	**120.00**
1911-D	55,700	**650.00**	1927	388,000	**120.00**
1912	616,200	**120.00**	1928	416,000	**120.00**
1913	722,200	**120.00**	1929	532,200	**120.00**
1914	240,100	**120.00**			

3 DOLLAR GOLD PIECES

Type: Liberty head with feather head-dress

(The mint marks are on the Rev., under the wreath)

Date	Amount Minted	Value	Date	Amount Minted	Value
1854	138,600	**400.00**	1856-S	34,500	**400.00**
1854-O	24,000	**400.00**	1857	20,900	**400.00**
1854-D	1,100	**4,000.00**	1857-S	14,000	**400.00**
1855	50,600	**400.00**	1858	2,100	**425.00**
1855-S	6,600	**400.00**	1859	15,600	**400.00**
1856	26,000	**400.00**	1860	7,200	**400.00**

Date	Amount Minted	Value	Date	Amount Minted	Value
1860-S	7,000	**400.00**	1875	About 50 proofs	**Rare**
1861	6,100	**400.00**	1876	About 50 proofs	**Rare**
1862	5,800	**400.00**	1877	1,500	**600.00**
1863	5,000	**400.00**	1878	82,300	**500.00**
1864	2,700	**525.00**	1879	3,000	**500.00**
1865	1,200	**600.00**	1880	1,000	**500.00**
1866	4,000	**400.00**	1881	550	**800.00**
1867	2,600	**400.00**	1882	1,500	**500.00**
1868	4,900	**400.00**	1883	900	**500.00**
1869	2,500	**400.00**	1884	1,100	**500.00**
1870	3,500	**400.00**	1885	900	**500.00**
1870-S	2	**Very Rare**	1886	1,100	**500.00**
1871	1,300	**500.00**	1887	6,200	**450.00**
1872	2,000	**400.00**	1888	5,300	**450.00**
1873	About 100 proofs	**Rare**	1889	2,400	**450.00**
1874	41,800	**400.00**			

4 DOLLAR GOLD PIECES (STELLAS)

Type: Liberty head with flowing hair.

1879	415 proofs	**14,000.00**	1880	15 proofs	**Rare**

Type: Liberty head with coiled hair.

1879	10 proofs	**Rare**	1880	10 proofs	**Rare**

5 DOLLAR GOLD PIECES (HALF EAGLES)

Type: Liberty head; with small eagle on Rev.

Date	*Amount Minted*	*Value*	*Date*	*Amount Minted*	*Value*
1795	Part of 8,700	**3,000.00**	1797	Part of 6,400	**3,500.00**
1796	3,400	**3,000.00**	1798	Part of 24,900	——

Type: Liberty head to right; with large eagle on Rev.

Date	Amount Minted	Value	Date	Amount Minted	Value
1795	Part of 8,700	**2,500.00**	1803	33,500	**800.00**
1797	Part of 6,400	**2,000.00**	1804	30,500	**800.00**
1798	Part of 24,900	**800.00**	1805	33,200	**800.00**
1799	7,500	**800.00**	1806	64,100	**800.00**
1800	11,600	**800.00**	1807	Part of 84,100	**800.00**
1802	53,200	**800.00**			

Type: Draped bust of Liberty to left with round cap.

Date	Amount Minted	Value	Date	Amount Minted	Value
1807	Part of 84,100	**800.00**	1810	100,300	**750.00**
1808	55,600	**750.00**	1811	99,600	**750.00**
1809	33,900	**750.00**	1812	58,100	**750.00**

Type: Liberty head with round cap; with motto over eagle.

Date	Amount Minted	Value	Date	Amount Minted	Value
1813	95,400	**900.00**	1825	29,100	**2,000.00**
1814	15,500	**1,000.00**	1826	18,100	**4,500.00**
1815	635	**Rare**	1827	24,900	**7,000.00**
1818	48,600	**900.00**	1828	28,000	**5,000.00**
1819	51,700	**Rare**	1829	57,400	**14,000.00**
1820	263,800	**900.00**	1830	126,400	**1,200.00**
1821	34,600	**2,000.00**	1831	140,600	**1,200.00**
1822 (3 known)	17,800	**Very Rare**	1832	157,500	**2,500.00**
1823	14,500	**1,500.00**	1833	193,600	**1,500.00**
1824	17,300	**3,500.00**	1834	Part of 732,200	**1,500.00**

Type: Liberty head with ribbon; without motto over eagle.

(The mint marks are on the Obv., over the date)

Date	Amount Minted	Value	Date	Amount Minted	Value
1834	Part of 732,200	**175.00**	1838	286,600	**175.00**
1835	371,500	**175.00**	1838-C	12,900	**700.00**
1836	553,100	**175.00**	1838-D	20,600	**700.00**
1837	207,100	**175.00**			

Type: Liberty head with coronet; without motto over eagle.

(The mint marks are on the Rev., under the eagle)

5 Dollar Gold Pieces (continued)

Date	*Amount Minted*	*Value*
1839	118,100	**130.00**
1839-C	23,500	**175.00**
1839-D	18,900	**175.00**
1840	137,400	**130.00**
1840-O	30,400	**130.00**
1840-C	19,000	**250.00**
1840-D	22,900	**300.00**
1841	15,800	**130.00**
1841-O	8,300	——
1841-C	21,500	**250.00**
1841-D	30,500	**250.00**
1842	27,600	**130.00**
1842-O	16,400	**200.00**
1842-C	27,500	**250.00**
1842-D	59,600	**250.00**
1843	611,200	**120.00**
1843-O	101,100	**130.00**
1843-C	44,400	**200.00**
1843-D	98,500	**200.00**
1844	340,300	**120.00**
1844-O	364,600	**130.00**
1844-C	23,600	**200.00**
1844-D	89,000	**200.00**
1845	417,100	**120.00**
1845-O	41,000	**130.00**
1845-D	90,600	**200.00**
1846	395,900	**120.00**
1846-O	58,000	**130.00**
1846-C	13,000	**300.00**
1846-D	80,300	**200.00**
1847	916,000	**120.00**
1847-O	12,000	**150.00**
1847-C	84,200	**250.00**
1847-D	64,400	**250.00**
1848	260,800	**120.00**
1848-C	64,500	**250.00**
1848-D	47,500	**250.00**
1849	133,100	**120.00**
1849-C	64,800	**250.00**
1849-D	39,000	**250.00**
1850	64,500	**120.00**
1850-C	63,600	**250.00**
1850-D	43,900	**250.00**
1851	377,500	**120.00**
1851-O	41,000	**130.00**
1851-C	49,200	**250.00**
1851-D	62,700	**250.00**
1852	573,900	**120.00**
1852-C	72,600	**250.00**
1852-D	91,500	**250.00**
1853	305,800	**120.00**
1853-C	65,600	**250.00**
1853-D	89,700	**250.00**
1854	160,700	**120.00**
1854-O	46,000	**130.00**
1854-C	39,300	**225.00**
1854-D	56,400	**225.00**
1854-S	268	——
1855	117,100	**120.00**
1855-O	11,100	**225.00**
1855-C	39,800	**225.00**
1855-D	22,400	**160.00**
1855-S	61,000	**130.00**
1856	198,000	**120.00**
1856-O	10,000	**250.00**
1856-C	28,500	**250.00**
1856-D	19,800	**250.00**
1856-S	105,100	**120.00**
1857	98,200	**120.00**
1857-O	13,000	**130.00**
1857-C	31,400	**250.00**
1857-D	17,000	**250.00**
1857-S	87,000	**130.00**
1858	15,100	**150.00**
1858-C	38,900	**250.00**
1858-D	15,400	**250.00**
1858-S	18,600	**130.00**
1859	16,800	**130.00**
1859-C	31,800	**250.00**
1859-D	10,400	**250.00**
1859-S	13,200	**130.00**
1860	19,800	**130.00**
1860-C	14,800	**250.00**
1860-D	14,600	**250.00**
1860-S	21,200	**130.00**
1861	639,900	**120.00**
1861-C	6,900	**900.00**
1861-D	1,600	**3,000.00**
1861-S	18,000	**130.00**
1862	4,500	**175.00**
1862-S	9,500	**130.00**
1863	2,500	**250.00**
1863-S	17,000	**130.00**
1864	4,200	**200.00**
1864-S	3,900	**800.00**
1865	1,300	**600.00**
1865-S	27,600	**225.00**
1866-S	Part of 43,900	**225.00**

Type: Liberty head with coronet; with motto over eagle.

(The mint marks are on the Rev., under the eagle)

Date	*Amount Minted*	*Value*	*Date*	*Amount Minted*	*Value*
1866	6,700	**175.00**	1879-CC	17,300	**225.00**
1866-S	Part of 43,900	**150.00**	1880	3¼ million	**110.00**
1867	6,900	**150.00**	1880-S	1⅓ million	**110.00**
1867-S	29,000	**120.00**	1880-CC	51,000	**225.00**
1868	5,700	**175.00**	1881	5⅔ million	**110.00**
1868-S	52,000	**110.00**	1881-S	969,000	**110.00**
1869	1,800	**400.00**	1881-CC	13,900	**225.00**
1869-S	31,000	**110.00**	1882	2½ million	**110.00**
1870	4,000	**150.00**	1882-S	970,000	**110.00**
1870-S	17,000	**140.00**	1882-CC	82,800	**150.00**
1870-CC	7,700	**1,500.00**	1883	233,400	**110.00**
1871	3,200	**175.00**	1883-S	83,200	**110.00**
1871-S	25,000	**110.00**	1883-CC	13,000	**225.00**
1871-CC	20,800	**500.00**	1884	191,000	**110.00**
1872	1,700	**400.00**	1884-S	177,000	**110.00**
1872-S	36,400	**110.00**	1884-CC	16,400	**225.00**
1872-CC	17,000	**190.00**	1885	601,500	**110.00**
1873	112,500	**110.00**	1885-S	1¼ million	**110.00**
1873-S	31,000	**110.00**	1886	388,400	**110.00**
1873-CC	7,400	**500.00**	1886-S	3¼ million	**110.00**
1874	3,500	**225.00**	1887	87 proofs	**Rare**
1874-S	16,000	**110.00**	1887-S	2 million	**110.00**
1874-CC	21,200	**250.00**	1888	18,300	**110.00**
1875	220	**Very Rare**	1888-S	293,900	**110.00**
1875-S	9,000	**150.00**	1889	7,600	**175.00**
1875-CC	11,800	**225.00**	1890	4,300	**190.00**
1876	1,500	**400.00**	1890-CC	53,800	**150.00**
1876-S	4,000	**600.00**	1891	61,400	**110.00**
1876-CC	6,900	**400.00**	1891-CC	208,000	**150.00**
1877	1,200	**400.00**	1892	753,600	**110.00**
1877-S	26,700	**110.00**	1892-O	10,000	**400.00**
1877-CC	8,700	**400.00**	1892-S	298,400	**110.00**
1878	131,700	**110.00**	1892-CC	83,000	**150.00**
1878-S	144,700	**110.00**	1893	1½ million	**110.00**
1878-CC	9,100	**1,100.00**	1893-O	110,000	**110.00**
1879	301,900	**110.00**	1893-S	224,000	**110.00**
1879-S	426,200	**110.00**	1893-CC	60,000	**150.00**

Date	Amount Minted	Value	Date	Amount Minted	Value
1894	958,000	**110.00**	1901-S	3⅔ million	**110.00**
1894-O	16,600	**150.00**	1902	172,600	**110.00**
1894-S	55,900	**110.00**	1902-S	939,000	**110.00**
1895	1⅓ million	**110.00**	1903	227,000	**110.00**
1895-S	112,000	**110.00**	1903-S	1¾ million	**110.00**
1896	59,100	**110.00**	1904	392,100	**110.00**
1896-S	155,400	**110.00**	1904-S	97,000	**110.00**
1897	867,900	**110.00**	1905	302,300	**110.00**
1897-S	354,000	**110.00**	1905-S	880,700	**110.00**
1898	633,500	**110.00**	1906	348,800	**110.00**
1898-S	1⅓ million	**110.00**	1906-S	598,000	**110.00**
1899	1¾ million	**110.00**	1906-D	320,000	**110.00**
1899-S	1½ million	**110.00**	1907	626,200	**110.00**
1900	1⅓ million	**110.00**	1907-D	888,000	**110.00**
1900-S	329,000	**110.00**	1908	421,900	**110.00**
1901	616,000	**110.00**			

Type: Indian head.

(The mint marks are on the Rev., to the left of the value)

Date	Amount Minted	Value	Date	Amount Minted	Value
1908	578,000	**140.00**	1911-S	1½ million	**140.00**
1908-D	148,000	**140.00**	1912	790,100	**140.00**
1908-S	82,000	**235.00**	1912-S	392,000	**140.00**
1909	627,100	**140.00**	1913	916,100	**140.00**
1909-O	34,200	**650.00**	1913-S	408,000	**140.00**
1909-D	3½ million	**140.00**	1914	247,100	**140.00**
1909-S	297,200	**140.00**	1914-D	247,000	**140.00**
1910	604,200	**140.00**	1914-S	263,000	**140.00**
1910-D	193,600	**140.00**	1915	588,100	**140.00**
1910-S	770,200	**140.00**	1915-S	164,000	**140.00**
1911	915,100	**140.00**	1916-S	240,000	**140.00**
1911-D	72,500	**250.00**	1929	662,000	**2,000.00**

The valuations listed in this book closely approximate how much established coin dealers will pay for any material needed in their stock.

10 DOLLAR GOLD PIECES (EAGLES)

Type: Liberty head; with small eagle on Rev.

Date	*Amount Minted*	*Value*	*Date*	*Amount Minted*	*Value*
1795	2,800	**5,000.00**	1797	Part of 9,200	**5,000.00**
1796	6,100	**5,000.00**			

Type: Liberty head; with large eagle on Rev.

Date	*Amount Minted*	*Value*	*Date*	*Amount Minted*	*Value*
1797	Part of 9,200	**1,300.00**	1801	29,300	**1,000.00**
1798	8,000	**2,000.00**	1803	9,000	**1,100.00**
1799	17,500	**1,000.00**	1804	9,800	**1,300.00**
1800	26,000	**1,100.00**			

Type: Liberty head; without motto on Rev.

(The mint marks are on the Rev., under the eagle)

Date	*Amount Minted*	*Value*	*Date*	*Amount Minted*	*Value*
1838	7,200	**400.00**	1840	47,300	**225.00**
1839	38,200	**300.00**	1841	63,100	**225.00**

Date	Amount Minted	Value	Date	Amount Minted	Value
1841-O	2,500	**250.00**	1855-O	18,000	**225.00**
1842	81,500	**225.00**	1855-S	9,000	**300.00**
1842-O	27,400	**225.00**	1856	60,500	**225.00**
1843	75,500	**225.00**	1856-O	14,500	**225.00**
1843-O	175,200	**225.00**	1856-S	68,000	**225.00**
1844	6,400	**250.00**	1857	16,600	**225.00**
1844-O	118,700	**225.00**	1857-O	5,500	**250.00**
1845	26,200	**225.00**	1857-S	26,000	**225.00**
1845-O	47,500	**225.00**	1858	2,500	**2,000.00**
1846	20,100	**225.00**	1858-O	20,000	**225.00**
1846-O	81,800	**225.00**	1858-S	11,800	**225.00**
1847	862,300	**225.00**	1859	16,100	**225.00**
1847-O	571,500	**225.00**	1859-O	2,300	**500.00**
1848	145,500	**225.00**	1859-S	7,000	**300.00**
1848-O	35,800	**225.00**	1860	11,800	**225.00**
1849	653,600	**225.00**	1860-O	11,100	**225.00**
1849-O	23,900	**225.00**	1860-S	5,000	**400.00**
1850	291,500	**225.00**	1861	113,200	**225.00**
1850-O	57,500	**225.00**	1861-S	15,500	**225.00**
1851	176,300	**225.00**	1862	11,000	**225.00**
1851-O	263,000	**225.00**	1862-S	12,500	**225.00**
1852	263,100	**225.00**	1863	1,200	**1,000.00**
1852-O	18,000	**225.00**	1863-S	10,000	**225.00**
1853	201,300	**225.00**	1864	3,600	**400.00**
1853-O	51,000	**225.00**	1864-S	2,500	**700.00**
1854	54,200	**225.00**	1865	4,000	**300.00**
1854-O	52,500	**225.00**	1865-S	16,700	**300.00**
1854-S	123,800	**225.00**	1866-S	Part of 20,000	**400.00**
1855	121,700	**225.00**			

Type: Liberty head; with motto on Rev.

(The mint marks are on the Rev., under the eagle)

Date	Amount Minted	Value	Date	Amount Minted	Value
1866	3,800	**225.00**	1869	1,900	**350.00**
1866-S	Part of 20,000	**225.00**	1869-S	6,400	**200.00**
1867	3,100	**225.00**	1870	2,500	**225.00**
1867-S	9,000	**225.00**	1870-S	8,000	**200.00**
1868	10,700	**200.00**	1870-CC	5,900	**450.00**
1868-S	13,500	**200.00**	1871	1,800	**225.00**

Date	*Amount Minted*	*Value*	*Date*	*Amount Minted*	*Value*
1871-S	16,500	**225.00**	1886-S	826,000	**175.00**
1871-CC	7,200	**350.00**	1887	53,700	**200.00**
1872	1,600	**400.00**	1887-S	817,000	**175.00**
1872-S	17,300	**225.00**	1888	133,000	**175.00**
1872-CC	5,500	**350.00**	1888-O	21,300	**200.00**
1873	825	**1000.00**	1888-S	648,700	**175.00**
1873-S	12,000	**225.00**	1889	4,500	**300.00**
1873-CC	4,500	**500.00**	1889-S	425,400	**175.00**
1874	53,200	**200.00**	1890	58,000	**200.00**
1874-S	10,000	**200.00**	1890-CC	17,500	**200.00**
1874-CC	16,800	**200.00**	1891	91,900	**175.00**
1875	120	—	1891-CC	103,700	**175.00**
1875-CC	7,700	**300.00**	1892	797,600	**175.00**
1876	732	**1,000.00**	1892-O	28,700	**175.00**
1876-S	5,000	**300.00**	1892-S	115,500	**175.00**
1876-CC	4,700	**400.00**	1892-CC	40,000	**225.00**
1877	817	**1,000.00**	1893	1¾ million	**175.00**
1877-S	17,000	**250.00**	1893-O	17,000	**200.00**
1877-CC	3,300	**500.00**	1893-S	141,300	**175.00**
1878	73,800	**200.00**	1893-CC	14,000	**200.00**
1878-S	26,100	**200.00**	1894	2½ million	**175.00**
1878-CC	3,200	**500.00**	1894-O	107,500	**175.00**
1879	384,800	**175.00**	1894-S	25,000	**200.00**
1879-O	1,500	**600.00**	1895	567,800	**175.00**
1879-S	224,000	**175.00**	1895-O	98,000	**175.00**
1879-CC	1,800	**1,000.00**	1895-S	49,000	**200.00**
1880	1⅔ million	**175.00**	1896	76,300	**200.00**
1880-O	9,200	**250.00**	1896-S	123,700	**200.00**
1880-S	506,200	**175.00**	1897	1 million	**175.00**
1880-CC	11,200	**225.00**	1897-O	42,500	**200.00**
1881	3¾ million	**175.00**	1897-S	234,700	**175.00**
1881-O	8,300	**225.00**	1898	812,200	**175.00**
1881-S	970,000	**175.00**	1898-S	473,600	**175.00**
1881-CC	24,000	**200.00**	1899	1¼ million	**175.00**
1882	2⅓ million	**175.00**	1899-O	37,000	**200.00**
1882-O	10,800	**200.00**	1899-S	841,000	**175.00**
1882-S	132,000	**200.00**	1900	294,000	**175.00**
1882-CC	6,800	**225.00**	1900-S	81,000	**200.00**
1883	208,700	**175.00**	1901	1¾ million	**175.00**
1883-O	800	**1,000.00**	1901-O	72,000	**200.00**
1883-S	38,000	**200.00**	1901-S	2¾ million	**175.00**
1883-CC	12,000	**225.00**	1902	82,500	**200.00**
1884	76,900	**200.00**	1902-S	469,500	**175.00**
1884-S	124,200	**175.00**	1903	125,900	**175.00**
1884-CC	9,900	**225.00**	1903-O	112,800	**175.00**
1885	253,500	**175.00**	1903-S	538,000	**175.00**
1885-S	228,000	**175.00**	1904	162,000	**175.00**
1886	236,200	**175.00**	1904-O	108,900	**175.00**

Date	*Amount Minted*	*Value*	*Date*	*Amount Minted*	*Value*
1905	201,000	**175.00**	1906-D	981,000	**175.00**
1905-S	369,200	**175.00**	1907	1¼ million	**175.00**
1906	165,500	**175.00**	1907-S	210,500	**175.00**
1906-O	86,900	**200.00**	1907-D	1 million	**175.00**
1906-S	457,000	**175.00**			

Type: Indian head; without motto on Rev.

(The Mint marks are on the Rev., to the left of the value. The "1907 Periods" indicates a period at each end of "United States of America" on the Rev.)

Date	Amount Minted	Value	Date	Amount Minted	Value
1907	239,400	**350.00**	1908	33,500	**375.00**
1907 Periods	542	**2,000.00**	1908-D	210,000	**350.00**

Type: Indian head; with motto on Rev.

Date	*Amount Minted*	*Value*
1908	341,500	**350.00**
1908-D	836,500	**350.00**
1908-S	59,900	**500.00**
1909	184,900	**350.00**
1909-D	121,500	**350.00**
1909-S	292,300	**350.00**
1910	318,700	**350.00**
1910-D	2⅓ million	**350.00**
1910-S	811,000	**350.00**
1911	505,600	**350.00**
1911-D	30,100	**400.00**
1911-S	51,000	**400.00**
1912	405,000	**350.00**
1912-S	300,000	**350.00**
1913	442,100	**350.00**
1913-S	66,000	**350.00**
1914	151,000	**350.00**
1914-D	343,500	**350.00**
1914-S	208,000	**350.00**
1915	351,100	**350.00**
1915-S	59,000	**400.00**
1916-S	138,500	**400.00**
1920-S	126,500	**4,500.00**
1926	1 million	**350.00**
1930-S	96,000	**2,500.00**
1932	4½ million	**350.00**
1933	312,500	—

20 DOLLAR GOLD PIECES (DOUBLE EAGLES)

Type: Liberty head; without motto on Rev.

(The mint marks are on the Rev., under the eagle)

Date	Amount Minted	Value	Date	Amount Minted	Value
1850	1¼ million	**525.00**	1858-O	35,200	**450.00**
1850-O	141,000	**450.00**	1858-S	846,700	**400.00**
1851	2 million	**400.00**	1859	43,600	**425.00**
1851-O	315,000	**425.00**	1859-O	9,100	**1,000.00**
1852	2 million	**400.00**	1859-S	636,400	**400.00**
1852-O	190,000	**425.00**	1860	577,700	**400.00**
1853	1¼ million	**400.00**	1860-O	6,600	**1,200.00**
1853-O	71,000	**550.00**	1860-S	544,900	**400.00**
1854	757,900	**400.00**	1861	3 million	**400.00**
1854-O	3,200	—	1861-O	5,000	**800.00**
1854-S	141,500	**400.00**	1861-S	768,000	**400.00**
1855	364,700	**400.00**	1862	92,100	**400.00**
1855-O	8,000	**900.00**	1862-S	854,200	**400.00**
1855-S	879,700	**400.00**	1863	142,800	**400.00**
1856	329,900	**400.00**	1863-S	966,600	**400.00**
1856-O	2,200	—	1864	204,300	**400.00**
1856-S	1¼ million	**400.00**	1864-S	793,700	**400.00**
1857	439,400	**400.00**	1865	351,200	**400.00**
1857-O	30,000	**400.00**	1865-S	1 million	**400.00**
1857-S	970,500	**400.00**	1866-S	Part of 842,200	**525.00**
1858	211,700	**400.00**			

Type: Liberty head; with motto on Rev. and "Twenty D."

(The mint marks are on the Rev., under the eagle)

Date	*Amount Minted*	*Value*	*Date*	*Amount Minted*	*Value*
1866	698,800	**375.00**	1872-S	780,000	**375.00**
1866-S	Part of 842,200	**375.00**	1872-CC	29,600	**550.00**
1867	251,065	**375.00**	1873	1¾ million	**375.00**
1867-S	920,700	**375.00**	1873-S	1 million	**375.00**
1868	98,600	**375.00**	1873-CC	22,400	**550.00**
1868-S	837,500	**375.00**	1874	366,800	**375.00**
1869	171,200	**375.00**	1874-S	1¼ million	**375.00**
1869-S	686,700	**375.00**	1874-CC	115,100	**400.00**
1870	155,200	**375.00**	1875	295,700	**375.00**
1870-S	982,000	**375.00**	1875-S	1¼ million	**375.00**
1870-CC	3,800	—	1875-CC	111,100	**400.00**
1871	80,100	**375.00**	1876	583,900	**375.00**
1871-S	928,000	**375.00**	1876-S	1½ million	**375.00**
1871-CC	14,700	**800.00**	1876-CC	138,400	**525.00**
1872	251,900	**375.00**			

Type: Liberty head; with motto on Rev. and "Twenty Dollars."

(The mint marks are on the Rev., under the eagle)

Date	*Amount Minted*	*Value*
1877	397,700	**375.00**
1877-S	1¾ million	**375.00**
1877-CC	42,600	**525.00**
1878	543,600	**375.00**
1878-S	1¾ million	**375.00**
1878-CC	13,200	**535.00**
1879	207,600	**375.00**
1879-O	2,300	**1,500.00**
1879-S	1¼ million	**375.00**
1879-CC	10,700	**550.00**
1880	51,500	**475.00**
1880-S	836,000	**375.00**
1881	2,300	**1,650.00**
1881-S	727,000	**375.00**
1882	630	**3,000.00**
1882-S	1¼ million	**375.00**
1882-CC	39,100	**500.00**
1883	About 100 proofs	—
1883-S	1¼ million	**375.00**
1883-CC	60,000	**500.00**
1884	71 proofs	—
1884-S	916,000	**375.00**
1884-CC	81,100	**500.00**
1885	828	**2,000.00**
1885-S	683,500	**375.00**
1885-CC	9,500	**550.00**
1886	1,100	**2,000.00**
1887	121 proofs	—
1887-S	283,000	**3,350.00**
1888	226,300	**375.00**
1888-S	859,600	**375.00**
1889	44,100	**375.00**
1889-S	774,700	**375.00**
1889-CC	30,900	**375.00**
1890	76,000	**375.00**
1890-S	802,700	**375.00**
1890-CC	91,200	**375.00**
1891	1,400	**1,000.00**
1891-S	1¼ million	**375.00**
1891-CC	5,000	**1,000.00**
1892	4,500	**700.00**
1892-S	930,100	**375.00**
1892-CC	27,300	**375.00**

Date	*Amount Minted*	*Value*	*Date*	*Amount Minted*	*Value*
1893	344,300	**375.00**	1901	111,500	**375.00**
1893-S	996,200	**375.00**	1901-S	1½ million	**375.00**
1893-CC	18,400	**375.00**	1902	31,300	**375.00**
1894	1⅓ million	**375.00**	1902-S	1¾ million	**375.00**
1894-S	1 million	**375.00**	1903	287,400	**375.00**
1895	1 million	**375.00**	1903-S	954,000	**375.00**
1895-S	1¼ million	**375.00**	1904	6¼ million	**375.00**
1896	792,700	**375.00**	1904-S	5¼ million	**375.00**
1896-S	1½ million	**375.00**	1905	59,000	**375.00**
1897	1⅓ million	**375.00**	1905-S	1¾ million	**375.00**
1897-S	1½ million	**375.00**	1906	69,700	**375.00**
1898	170,500	**375.00**	1906-S	2 million	**375.00**
1898-S	2½ million	**375.00**	1906-D	620,200	**375.00**
1899	1⅔ million	**375.00**	1907	1½ million	**375.00**
1899-S	2 million	**375.00**	1907-S	2¼ million	**375.00**
1900	1¾ million	**375.00**	1907-D	842,200	**375.00**
1900-S	2½ million	**375.00**			

Type: Liberty standing (St. Gaudens design). Date in Roman Numerals, MCMVII.

1907	11,200	**2,000.00**

Type: Liberty standing; date in normal numerals; without motto on Rev.

(The mint mark is on the Obv., over the date)

Date	*Amount Minted*	*Value*	*Date*	*Amount Minted*	*Value*
1907	361,700	**550.00**	1908-D	663,700	**450.00**
1908	4¼ million	**450.00**			

Type: Liberty standing; with motto on Rev.

(The mint marks are on the Obv., over the date)

Date	Amount Minted	Value	Date	Amount Minted	Value
1908	156,400	**425.00**	1914	95,300	**425.00**
1908-D	349,500	**425.00**	1914-D	453,000	**425.00**
1908-S	22,000	**650.00**	1914-S	1½ million	**425.00**
1909	Part of 161,300	**425.00**	1915	152,000	**450.00**
1909 over 8	Part of 161,300	**450.00**	1915-S	567,500	**450.00**
1909-D	52,500	**550.00**	1916-S	796,000	**450.00**
1909-S	2¾ million	**425.00**	1920	228,200	**450.00**
1910	482,200	**425.00**	1920-S	558,000	**4,500.00**
1910-D	429,000	**425.00**	1921	528,500	**6,500.00**
1910-S	2¼ million	**425.00**	1922	1⅓ million	**425.00**
1911	197,300	**425.00**	1922-S	2⅔ million	**550.00**
1911-D	846,500	**425.00**	1923	566,000	**425.00**
1911-S	775,700	**425.00**	1923-D	1⅔ million	**425.00**
1912	149,800	**425.00**	1924	4⅓ million	**425.00**
1913	168,800	**425.00**	1924-D	3 million	**725.00**
1913-D	393,500	**425.00**	1924-S	3 million	**675.00**
1913-S	34,000	**425.00**	1925	2¾ million	**425.00**

Date	*Amount Minted*	*Value*	*Date*	*Amount Minted*	*Value*
1925-D	3 million	**650.00**	1928	8¾ million	**450.00**
1925-S	3¾ million	**600.00**	1929	1¾ million	**2,000.00**
1926	816,700	**425.00**	1930-S	74,000	**3,000.00**
1926-D	481,000	**650.00**	1931	3 million	**4,000.00**
1926-S	2 million	**525.00**	1931-D	106,500	**4,500.00**
1927	3 million	**425.00**	1932	1 million	**4,000.00**
1927-D	180,000	—	1933	445,500	**not issued**
1927-S	3 million	**2,000.00**			

Pioneer Gold Coins

Coinage of the Territorial and Private Mints

(The valuations are for coins in VG to F condition)
(Beware of Copies)

BALDWIN & CO.

San Francisco, California

Horseman with lariat. Rev. Eagle.

10 Dollars 1850 .... **6,500.00**

"Baldwin & Co" on head band of Liberty. Rev. Eagle.

5 Dollars 1850 .... **1,500.00**
10 Dollars 1851 .... **4,000.00**
20 Dollars 1851 .... —

AUGUST BECHTLER

Rutherford, North Carolina

Value and legend. Rev. Weight and legend. The coins are undated but were struck from 1842 to 1852.

1 Dollar ND. One variety	350.00
5 Dollars ND. Three varieties	950.00

CHRISTOPHER BECHTLER

Rutherford, North Carolina

Value and legend. Rev. Weight and legend. The coins are undated, but were struck from 1831 to 1842.

1 Dollar ND. Four varieties	400.00
2½ Dollars ND. Seven varieties	750.00
5 Dollars ND. Six varieties	950.00
5 Dollars August 1, 1834. Two varieties	950.00

The valuations listed in this book closely approximate how much established coin dealers will pay for any material needed in their stock.

EPHRAIM BRASHER

New York

Radiant sun over mountains. Rev. Eagle with "EB" punched on either the wing or breast. The famous Brasher Doubloon.

Doubloon 1787 Extremely Rare .... —
½ Doubloon 1787 Extremely Rare .... —

CINCINNATI MINING & TRADING CO.

San Francisco, California

Indian Head. Rev. Eagle

5 Dollars 1849 .... —
10 Dollars 1849 .... —

CLARK, GRUBER & CO.

Denver, Colorado

View of Pikes Peak. Rev. Eagle

10 Dollars 1860 .... 1,000.00
20 Dollars 1860 .... 5,000.00

"Clark & Co." on head band of Liberty. Rev. Eagle.

2½	Dollars 1860	350.00
5	Dollars 1860	500.00

"Pikes Peak" on head band of Liberty. Rev. Eagle.

2½	Dollars 1861	400.00
5	Dollars 1861	500.00
10	Dollars 1861	500.00
20	Dollars 1861	1,250.00

J. J. CONWAY & CO.

Georgia Gulch, Colorado

Name of company. Rev. Value and "Pikes Peak."
Undated but struck in 1861.

2½	Dollars ND	—
5	Dollars ND	—
10	Dollars ND	—

DUBOSQ & CO.

San Francisco, California

"Dubosq & Co." on head band of Liberty. Rev. Eagle.

5 Dollars 1850	—
10 Dollars 1850	—

DUNBAR & CO.

San Francisco, California

"Dunbar & Co." on head band of Liberty. Rev. Eagle.

5 Dollars 1851	—

AUGUSTUS HUMBERT

U.S. Assayer of gold, San Francisco, California

Eagle. Rev. Four line legend in tablet.

10 Dollars 1852	**750.00**
20 Dollars 1852	**1,250.00**

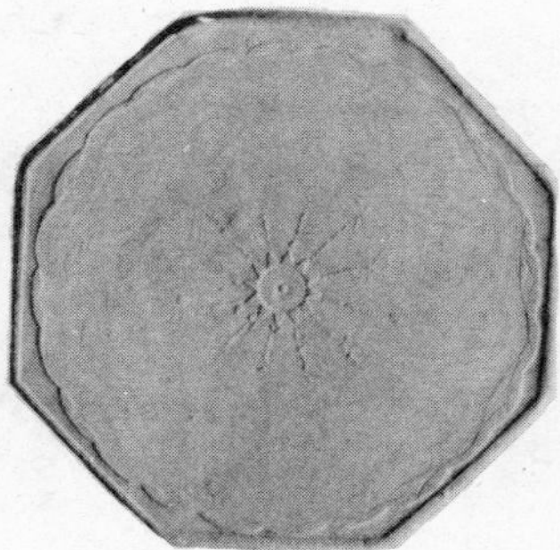

Eagle. Rev. Small 50, star or circle in center of otherwise blank Rev. Octagonal shaped with lettered edge.

50 Dollars 1851. Five varieties 3,500.00

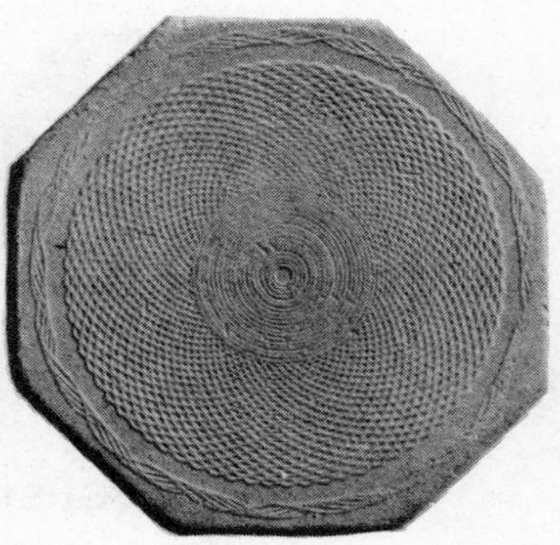

Eagle. Rev. Machine made criss-cross of circular lines. Octagonal shaped with reeded edge.

50 Dollars 1851, 52. Three varieties 3,500.00

KELLOGG & CO.

San Francisco, California

"Kellogg & Co." on head band of Liberty. Rev. Standard Eagle.

20 Dollars 1854, 55 .... **700.00**

Obv. Similar to above. Rev. Eagle holding shield.

50 Dollars 1855 .... —

MASSACHUSETTS & CALIFORNIA CO.

San Francisco, California

Arms supported by bear and stag. Value in wreath.

5 Dollars 1849. Four varieties .... —

MINERS BANK

San Francisco, California

Name and value. Rev. Eagle.

10 Dollars 1849 . . . . 2,000.00

MOFFAT & CO.

San Francisco, California

"Moffat & Co." on head band of Liberty. Rev. Eagle.

5 Dollars 1849, 50 . . . . 300.00
10 Dollars 1849, 52 . . . . 650.00
20 Dollars 1853 . . . . 800.00

THE MORMONS

Salt Lake City, Utah

Eye and Bishop's Mitre. Rev. Clasped hands.

2½ Dollars 1849 . . . . 1,200.00
5 Dollars 1849, 50 . . . . 1,000.00
10 Dollars 1849 . . . . ——
20 Dollars 1849 . . . . ——

Lion. Rev. Beehive on breast of eagle.

5 Dollars 1860 .... **2,000.00**

NORRIS, GRIEG & NORRIS

San Francisco, California

Eagle. Rev. Legend.

5 Dollars 1849. Plain or reeded edge **950.00**

OREGON EXCHANGE CO.

Oregon City, Oregon

Beaver and initials. Rev. Legend.

5 Dollars 1849 .... 2,500.00
10 Dollars 1849 .... 9,000.00

J. S. ORMSBY

San Francisco, California

"J. S. O." Rev. Value. Undated but struck in 1849.

5 Dollars ND .... —
10 Dollars ND .... —

PACIFIC CO.

San Francisco, California

Liberty Cap. Rev. Eagle.

5 Dollars 1849 .... —
10 Dollars 1849 .... —

JOHN PARSONS & CO.

Tarryall Mines, Colorado

Stamping machine. Rev. Eagle and "Pikes Peak Gold." Undated but struck in 1861.

2½ Dollars ND .... —
5 Dollars ND, ... —

SHULTS & CO.

San Francisco, California

"Shults & Co." on head band of Liberty. Rev. Eagle.

5 Dollars 1851	4,000.00

TEMPLETON REID

Lumpkin County, Georgia

Legend on each side.

2½	Dollars 1830	—
5	Dollars 1830	—
10	Dollars 1830	—
10	Dollars ND	—

TEMPLETON REID

San Francisco, California

Legend on each side.

10 Dollars 1849	—
25 Dollars 1849	—

UNITED STATES ASSAY OFFICE OF GOLD

San Francisco, California

Eagle. Rev. Legend in tablet.

10 Dollars 1852, 53. Two varieties 500.00
20 Dollars 1853. Two varieties 950.00

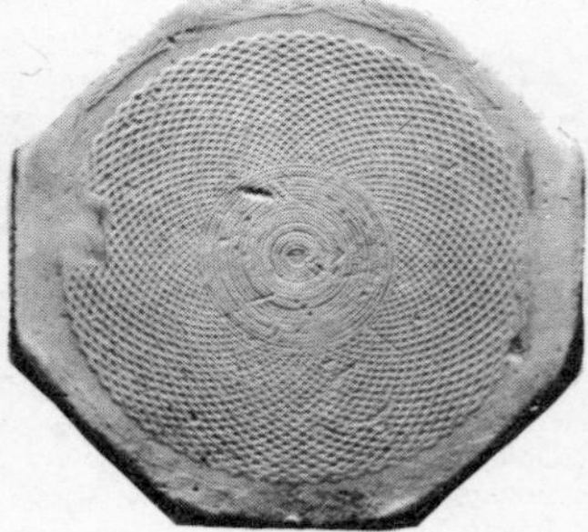

Eagle. Rev. Machine made criss-cross of circular lines. Octagonal shaped.

50 Dollars 1852. Two varieties 2,500.00

WASS, MOLITOR & CO.

San Francisco, California

"W.M. & Co." on head band of Liberty. Rev. Eagle.

5 Dollars 1852 .... 1,200.00
10 Dollars 1852, 55. Two varieties 1,000.00
20 Dollars. 1855. Two varieties 2,750.00

Liberty head. Rev. Name and value.
50 Dollars 1855 .... **5,000.00**

United States Proof Sets

(1936 to date)

A Proof Set contains five coins; the 1c, 5c, 25c, and 50c pieces. From 1936 through 1942, unequal amounts were struck of each denomination; from 1950 to date equal amounts have been struck. In the column under Amount Minted, the figure shows the total number of *complete* sets minted in each year. In 1942, two types of proof 5 Cent pieces were struck, the standard coin and the one with silver content; hence, there are two listings for the 1942 Proof Set. In 1973 and 1974, the dollar was added to the set. In 1975, the Proof Set contained the 1975-S 1c, 5c and 10c pieces plus the 1976-S Bicentennial 25c, 50c and dollar. Because of speculation, the valuations are subject to fluctuation.

Year	*Amount Minted*	***Value***
1936	3,837	**3,500.00**
1937	5,542	**2,500.00**
1938	8,045	**1,200.00**
1939	8,795	**1,100.00**
1940	11,246	**800.00**
1941	15,287	**700.00**
1942 with one nickel	21,120	
1942 with two nickels		**700.00**
1950	51,386	**375.00**
1951	57,500	**225.00**
1952	81,980	**130.00**
1953	128,800	**75.00**
1954	233,300	**40.00**
1955	378,200	**42.50**
1956	669,384	**21.00**
1957	1,247,952	**13.00**
1958	875,652	**20.00**
1959	1,149,291	**13.50**
1960 small date	1,691,600	**14.00**
1960 large date		**11.50**
1961	3,028,244	**9.50**
1962	3,218,039	**9.50**
1963	3,075,645	**9.50**
1964	3,949,634	**11.00**
1965 special mint set	2,360,000	**6.00**
1966 special mint set	2,261,583	**4.50**
1967 special mint set	1,863,344	**6.50**
1968 proof set	3,041,509	**3.50**
1969	2,934,631	**3.50**
1970 small date	2,632,810	**40.00**
1970 large date		**7.00**
1971	3,224,138	**3.00**
1972	3,267,667	**3.00**
1973	2,769,624	**5.00**
1974	2,617,350	**4.00**
1975	2,845,451	**6.00**
1976 3-pc. set	3,295,715	**9.50**
1976	4,149,730	**4.00**
1977	3,251,152	**3.75**
1978	3,127,781	**4.00**
1979 Type I	3,677,175	**7.50**
1979 Type II		**60.00**
1980	3,547,030	**5.00**
1981 Type I	4,063,083	**5.00**
1981 Type II		**100.00**
1982	3,857,479	**4.00**
1983	3,183,765	**8.00**
1983 Prestige		**60.00**
1984		**12.00**
1984 Prestige		**37.50**
1985		**12.50**
1986		**12.00**
1986 Prestige		**27.50**
1987		**9.00**
1987 Prestige		**22.50**
1988		**7.00**
1988 Prestige		**30.00**

United States Paper Money

(1861 to date)

Large Size Notes, Small Size Notes, Fractional Currency

1 DOLLAR NOTES

Torn, frayed or excessively worn notes command little or no premium.

All modern Federal Reserve Notes after 1974 have no premium.

Type of Issue	*Series*	*Portrait or Main Design*	*Value*
LARGE SIZE NOTES			**USED CONDITION**
U.S. Note (Legal Tender)	1862	Chase	**20.00**
"	1869	Washington	**25.00**
"	1874	Washington	**15.00**
"	1875	Washington	**9.00**
"	1878	Washington	**9.00**
"	1880	Washington	**10.00**
"	1917	Washington	**5.00**
"	1923	Washington (Red Seal)	**7.50**
Silver Certificate	1886	Martha Washington	**16.00**
"	1891	Martha Washington	**15.00**
"	1896	George and Martha Washington (on Rev.)	**20.00**
"	1899	Lincoln and Grant	**4.50**
"	1923	Washington (Blue Seal)	**3.00**
Treasury or Coin Note	1890	Stanton	**20.00**
"	1891	Stanton	**10.00**
National Bank Note	Old (original)	Two maidens standing	**30.00**
"	1875	Two maidens standing	**30.00**
Federal Reserve Bank Note	1918	Washington	**4.50**
SMALL SIZE NOTES			**NEW CONDITION**
U.S. Note (Red Seal)	1928	Washington	**20.00**
Silver Certificate (Blue Seal)	1928 (A-E)	Washington	**3.50**
"	1934	Washington	**2.50**
Silver Certificate (Blue Seal)	1935 (A-H*)	Washington	**1.20**
"	1957 (A-B)	Washington	**1.10**
Hawaiian Issue (Brown Seal)	1935-A	Washington	**10.00**
Armed Forces Issue (Yellow Seal)	1935-A	Washington	**12.00**
Federal Reserve (Green Seal)	1963 (A-B)	Washington	**1.00**
"	1969 (A-D)	Washington	**1.00**
"	1974 & later	Washington	**Current**

*1935-G with and without motto

2 DOLLAR NOTES

Torn, frayed or excessively worn notes command little or no premium.

All modern Federal Reserve Notes after 1974 have no premium.

Type of Issue	*Series*	*Portrait or Main Design*	*Value*
LARGE SIZE NOTES			**USED CONDITION**
U.S. Note (Legal Tender)	1862	Hamilton	**20.00**
"	1869	Jefferson	**22.50**
"	1874	Jefferson	**20.00**
"	1875	Jefferson	**17.50**
"	1878	Jefferson	**17.50**
"	1880	Jefferson	**10.00**
"	1917	Jefferson	**5.00**

Type of Issue	Series	Portrait or Main Design	Value
LARGE SIZE NOTES			**USED CONDITION**
Silver Certificate	1886	Gen. Hancock	**24.00**
"	1891	William Windom	**22.50**
"	1896	Fulton and Morse (on Rev.)	**32.00**
"	1899	Washington	**12.00**
Treasury or Coin Note	1890	Gen. McPherson	**35.00**
"	1891	Gen. McPherson	**20.00**
National Bank Note	Old (original)	Large, horizontal "lazy" 2	**100.00**
"	1875	Large, horizontal "lazy" 2	**100.00**
Federal Reserve Bank Note	1918	Jefferson	**12.00**
SMALL SIZE NOTES			**NEW CONDITION**
U.S. Note	1928 (A-G)	Jefferson	**4.00**
"	1953 (A-C)	Jefferson	**2.25**
"	1963 (A)	Jefferson	**2.10**
Federal Reserve Note	1976	Jefferson	**2.00**

5 DOLLAR NOTES

Torn, frayed or excessively worn notes command little or no premium.
All modern Federal Reserve Notes after 1974 have no premium.

Type of Issue	Series	Portrait or Main Design	Value
LARGE SIZE NOTES			**USED CONDITION**
Demand Note	1861	Hamilton	**150.00**
U.S. Note (Legal Tender)	1862	Hamilton	**17.00**
"	1863	Hamilton	**17.00**
"	1869	Jackson	**22.00**
"	1875	Jackson	**15.00**
"	1878	Jackson	**12.00**
"	1880	Jackson	**10.00**
"	1907	Jackson	**10.00**
Silver Certificate	1886	Grant	**70.00**
"	1891	Grant	**35.00**
"	1896	Grant and Sheridan (on Rev.)	**65.00**
"	1899	Indian Chief, Onepapa	**40.00**
"	1923	Lincoln	**45.00**
Treasury or Coin Note	1890	Gen. Thomas	**32.00**
"		Gen. Thomas	**30.00**
National Bank Note	Old (original)	Landing of Columbus (on Rev.)	**25.00**
"	1875	Landing of Columbus (on Rev.)	**25.00**
"	1882	Garfield; brown back	**15.00**
"	1882	Garfield; "1882-1908" on back	**15.00**
"	1882	Garfield; "Five Dollars" on back	**18.00**
"	1902	Harrison; red seal	**11.00**
"	1902	Harrison; blue seal; "1902-1908" on back	**7.00**
"	1902	Harrison; blue seal only	**7.00**
Federal Reserve Bank Note	1915	Lincoln	**9.00**
"	1918	Lincoln	**9.00**
Federal Reserve Note	1914	Lincoln; red seal	**12.00**
"	1914	Lincoln; blue seal	**6.00**
National Gold Bank Note	1870-74	Gold coins on bank	**200.00**

Type of Issue	*Series*	*Portrait or Main Design*	*Value*
SMALL SIZE NOTES			**NEW CONDITION**
U.S. Note	1928 (A-F)	Lincoln	**6.50**
"	1953 (A-C)	Lincoln	**5.50**
"	1963	Lincoln	**5.10**
Silver Certificate	1934 (A-D)	Lincoln	**6.00**
"	1953 (A-B)	Lincoln	**5.25**
National Bank Note	1929	Lincoln	**15.00**
Federal Reserve Bank Note	1929	Lincoln	**10.00**
Federal Reserve Note	1928 (A-D)	Lincoln	**8.00**
"	1934 (A-D)	Lincoln	**5.25**
"	1950 (A-E)	Lincoln	**5.00**
"	1963 (A)	Lincoln	**5.00**
"	1969 (A-C)	Lincoln	**5.00**
"	1974 & later	Lincoln	**Current**
Hawaiian Issue (Brown Seal)	1934 (A)	Lincoln	**28.00**
Armed Forces Issue (Yellow Seal)	1934-A	Lincoln	**20.00**

10 DOLLAR NOTES

Torn, frayed or excessively worn notes command little or no premium.

All modern Federal Reserve Notes after 1974 have no premium.

LARGE SIZE NOTES			**USED CONDITION**
Demand Note	1861	Lincoln	**275.00**
U.S. Note (Legal Tender)	1862	Lincoln	**40.00**
"	1863	Lincoln	**40.00**
"	1869	Webster	**45.00**
"	1875	Webster	**30.00**
U.S. Note (Legal Tender)	1878	Webster	**30.00**
"	1880	Webster	**17.00**
"	1901	Lewis and Clark; bison	**40.00**
"	1923	Jackson	**70.00**
Compound Interest Note	1863-65	Chase	**175.00**
Interest Bearing Note (one year)	1864	Chase	**375.00**
Refunding Certificate	1879	Franklin	**140.00**
Silver Certificate	1878	Robert Morris	**500.00**
"	1880	Robert Morris	**70.00**
"	1886	Thomas Hendricks	**50.00**
"	1891	Thomas Hendricks	**22.00**
"	1908	Thomas Hendricks	**20.00**
Treasury or Coin Note	1890	Gen. Sheridan	**50.00**
"	1891	Gen. Sheridan	**30.00**
National Bank Note	Old (original)	De Soto at the Mississippi (on Rev.)	**40.00**
"	1875	De Soto at the Mississippi (on Rev.)	**40.00**
"	1882	Franklin with kite; brown back	**25.00**
"	1882	Same with "1882-1908" on back	**25.00**
"	1882	Same with "Ten Dollars" on back	**28.00**
"	1902	McKinley; red seal	**20.00**
"	1902	McKinley; blue seal; "1902-1908" on back	**12.00**
"	1902	McKinley; blue seal only	**12.00**

Type of Issue	Series	Portrait or Main Design	Value
LARGE SIZE NOTES			**USED CONDITION**
Federal Reserve Bank Note	1915	Jackson	**22.50**
"	1918	Jackson	**22.50**
Federal Reserve Note	1914	Jackson; red seal	**13.00**
"	1914	Jackson; blue seal	**11.00**
National Gold Bank Note	1870-75	Gold coins on back	**250.00**
Gold Certificate	1907	Michael Hillegas	**13.00**
"	1922	Michael Hillegas	**13.00**
SMALL SIZE NOTES			**NEW CONDITION**
Silver Certificate	1933	Hamilton	**1,200.00**
"	1934 (A-D)	Hamilton	**12.00**
"	1953 (A-B)	Hamilton	**11.00**
National Bank Note	1929	Hamilton	**20.00**
Federal Reserve Bank Note	1929	Hamilton	**12.00**
Federal Reserve Note	1928 (A-C)	Hamilton	**10.50**
"	1934 (A-D)	Hamilton	**10.00**
"	1950 (A-E)	Hamilton	**10.00**
"	1963 (A)	Hamilton	**10.00**
"	1969 (A-C)	Hamilton	**10.00**
"	1974 & later	Hamilton	**Current**
Hawaiian Issue (Brown Seal)	1934-A	Hamilton	**35.00**
Armed Forces Issue (Yellow Seal)	1934 (A)	Hamilton	**30.00**
Gold Certificate	1928	Hamilton	**45.00**

20 DOLLAR NOTES

Torn, frayed or excessively worn notes command little or no premium.
All modern Federal Reserve Notes after 1974 have no premium.

LARGE SIZE NOTES			**USED CONDITION**
Demand Note	1861	Liberty Standing	**1,200.00**
U.S. Note (Legal Tender)	1862	Liberty Standing	**45.00**
"	1863	Liberty Standing	**45.00**
"	1869	Hamilton	**100.00**
"	1875	Hamilton	**30.00**
"	1878	Hamilton	**25.00**
"	1880	Hamilton	**22.50**
Compound Interest Note	1863–65	Lincoln	**400.00**
Interest Bearing Note (one year)	1864	Lincoln	**750.00**
Silver Certificate	1878	Stephen Decatur	**600.00**
"	1880	Stephen Decatur	**125.00**
"	1886	Daniel Manning	**100.00**
"	1891	Daniel Manning	**30.00**
Treasury or Coin Note	1890	John Marshall	**100.00**
"	1891	John Marshall	**120.00**
National Bank Note	Old (original)	Baptism of Pocahontas (on Rev.)	**60.00**
"	1875	Baptism of Pocahontas (on Rev.)	**60.00**
"	1882	Battle of Lexington; brown back	**28.00**
"	1882	Same with "1882-1908" on back	**28.00**
"	1882	Same with "Twenty Dollars" on back	**32.00**
"	1902	Hugh McCulloch; red seal	**25.00**
"	1902	Hugh McCulloch; blue seal; "1902-1908" on back	**22.00**

Type of Issue	Series	Portrait or Main Design	Value
LARGE SIZE NOTES			**USED CONDITION**
National Bank Note	1902	Huch McCulloch; blue seal only	22.00
Federal Reserve Bank Note	1915	Cleveland	40.00
"	1918	Cleveland	40.00
Federal Reserve Note	1914	Cleveland; red seal	25.00
"	1914	Cleveland; blue seal	22.00
National Gold Bank Note	1870–75	Gold coins on back	400.00
Gold Certificate	1863	Eagle on shield	——
"	1882	Garfield	32.00
"	1905	Washington	70.00
"	1906	Washington	27.00
"	1922	Washington	27.00
SMALL SIZE NOTES			**NEW CONDITION**
National Bank Note	1929	Jackson	30.00
Federal Reserve Bank Note	1929	Jackson	22.00
Federal Reserve Note	1928 (A–C)	Jackson	21.00
"	1934 (A–D)	Jackson	20.00
"	1950 (A–E)	Jackson	20.00
"	1963 (A)	Jackson	20.00
"	1969 (A–C)	Jackson	20.00
"	1974 & later	Jackson	Current
Hawaiian Issue (Brown Seal)	1934 (A)	Jackson	50.00
Gold Certificate	1928	Jackson	50.00

50 DOLLAR NOTES

Torn, frayed or excessivley worn notes command little or no premium.

All modern Federal Reserve Notes after 1974 have no premium.

Type of Issue	Series	Portrait or Main Design	Value
LARGE SIZE NOTES			**USED CONDITION**
U.S. Note (Legal Tender)	1862	Hamilton	375.00
"	1863	Hamilton	375.00
"	1869	Henry Clay	700.00
"	1874	Franklin	165.00
"	1875	Franklin	150.00
"	1878	Franklin	150.00
"	1880	Franklin	70.00
Compound Interest Note	1863–65	Hamilton	Rare
Interest Bearing Note (one year)	1864	Hamilton	Rare
Interest Bearing Note (two years)	1863	Three females	Rare
Interest Bearing Note (three years)	1861	Large eagle	Rare
"	1864	Large eagle	Rare
"	1865	Large eagle	Rare
"	1865	Large eagle	Rare
Silver Certificate	1878	Edward Everett	650.00
"	1880	Edward Everett	700.00
"	1891	Edward Everett	85.00
Treasury or Coin Note	1891	William Seward	1,200.00
National Bank Note	Old (original)	Embarkation of the Pilgrims (on Rev.)	450.00
"	1875	Embarkation of the Pilgrims (on Rev.)	450.00
"	1882	Washington Crossing the Delaware and at prayer; brown back	75.00
"	1882	Same with "1882-1908" on back	75.00

Type of Issues	*Series*	*Portrait or Main Design*	*Value*
SMALL SIZE NOTES			**USED CONDITION**
Federal Reserve Bank Note	1929	Grant	**51.00**
Federal Reserve Note	1928(A)	Grant	**50.00**
"	1934(A–D)	Grant	**50.00**
"	1950(A–E)	Grant	**50.00**
"	1963-A	Grant	**50.00**
"	1969(A–C)	Grant	**50.00**
"	1974 & later	Grant	**Current**
Gold Certificate	1928	Grant	**150.00**

100 DOLLAR NOTES

Torn, frayed or excessively worn notes command little or no premium

All modern Federal Reserve Notes after 1974 have no premium.

LARGE SIZE NOTES			**USED CONDITION**
U.S. Note (Legal Tender)	1862	Large eagle	**600.00**
"	1863	Large eagle	**600.00**
"	1869	Lincoln	**1,000.00**
"	1875	Lincoln	**650.00**
"	1878	Lincoln	**650.00**
"	1880	Lincoln	**175.00**
Compound Interest Note	1863–65	Washington standing	**700.00**
Interest Bearing Note (one year)	1864	Washington standing	**Rare**
Interest Bearing Note (two years)	1863	Agriculture and Industry	**Rare**
Interest Bearing Note (three years)	1861	Gen. Scott	**Rare**
"	1865	Gen. Scott	**Rare**
Silver Certificate	1878	Monroe	**800.00**
"	1880	Monroe	**700.00**
"	1891	Monroe	**325.00**
Treasury or Coin Note	1890	Commodore Farragut	**1,000.00**
"	1891	Commodore Farragut	**1,000.00**
National Bank Note	Old (original)	Signing of the Declaration of Independence (on Rev.)	**400.00**
"	1875	Signing the Declaration of Independence (on Rev.)	**400.00**
"	1882	Commodore Perry leaving his flagship; brown back	**125.00**
"	1882	Same with "1882–1908" on back	**120.00**
"	1882	Same with "One Hundred Dollars" on back	**Rare**
"	1902	John Knox; red seal	**110.00**
"	1902	John Knox; blue seal; "1902 1908" on back	**100.00**
"	1902	John Knox; blue seal only	**100.00**
Federal Reserve Note	1914	Franklin; red seal	**100.00**
"	1914	Franklin; blue seal	**100.00**
National Gold Bank Note	1870–75	Gold coins on back	**2,000.00**
Gold certificate	1863	Eagle on shield	—
"	1870–71	Thomas Benton	—
"	1875	Thomas Benton	—
"	1882	Thomas Benton	**110.00**
"	1922	Thomas Benton	**125.00**

Type of Issues	Series	Portrait or Main Design	Value
SMALL SIZE NOTES			**NEW CONDITION**
National Bank Note	1929	Franklin	100.00
Federal Reserve Bank Note	1929	Franklin	100.00
Federal Reserve Note	1928 (A)	Franklin	100.00
"	1934 (A-D)	Franklin	100.00
"	1950 (A-E)	Franklin	100.00
"	1963-A	Franklin	100.00
"	1969 (A-C)	Franklin	100.00
"	1974 & later	Franklin	Current
U.S. Note (Legal Tender)	1966 (A)	Franklin	100.00
Gold Certificate	1928	Franklin	150.00

Fractional Currency

Torn, frayed or excessively worn notes command little or no premium.

3 CENT NOTES

Years of Issue	Description	Used
1864-1869	Small head of Washington.	3.00

5 CENT NOTES

Years of Issue	Description	Used
1862-1863	Facsimile of a 5 Cent postage stamp with head of Jefferson	2.00
1862-1863	Same as above but with perforated edges.	2.50
1863-1867	Head of Washington in bronze oval frame. Brown back.	1.50
1864-1869	Head of Spencer M. Clark. Green back.	1.50
1864-1869	Same as above but with red back.	2.00

10 CENT NOTES

Years of Issue	*Description*	*Used*
1862-1863	Facsimile of a 10 Cent postage stamp with head of Washington.	**2.00**
1862-1863	Same as above but with perforated edges.	**2.50**
1863-1867	Head of Washington in bronze oval frame. Green back.	**1.50**
1864-1869	Head of Washington. A bronze "10" in each corner. Green back.	**1.50**
1864-1869	Same as above but with red back.	**2.50**
1869-1875	Bust of Liberty.	**1.25**
1874-1876	Head of William M. Meredith. Green seal.	**1.25**
1874-1876	Same as above but with red seal.	**1.00**

15 CENT NOTES

1869-1875	Bust of Columbia.	**3.50**
Not Issued	Heads of Grant and Sherman. Separate front and back. Green back.	**20.00**
Not Issued	Same as above but with red back.	**20.00**

25 CENT NOTES

1862-1863	Facsimiles of five 5 Cent postage stamps with head of Jefferson.	**3.00**
1862-1863	Same as above but with perforated edges.	**4.00**
1863-1867	Head of Washington in bronze oval frame. Purple back.	**1.75**
1864-1869	Bust of Fessenden. Green back.	**1.75**
1864-1869	Same as above but with red back.	**3.00**
1869-1875	Bust of Washington.	**1.25**
1874-1876	Bust of Robert V. Walker.	**.75**

50 CENT NOTES

1862-1863	Facsimiles of five 10 Cent postage stamps with head of Washington.	**3.00**
1862-1863	Same as above but with perforated edges.	**5.00**
1863-1867	Head of Washington in bronze oval frame. Red back.	**1.75**
1864-1869	Bust of Gen. Spinner. Green back with a "50" at each end.	**1.75**
1864-1869	Same as above but with red back.	**2.00**
1864-1869	Bust of Gen. Spinner. Green back with "50" in center.	**1.75**
1864-1869	Seated figure of Justice. Green back.	**2.00**
1864-1869	Same as above but with red back.	**2.00**
1869-1875	Bust of Lincoln.	**4.00**
1869-1875	Bust of E. M. Stanton.	**2.00**
1869-1875	Bust of Samuel Dexter.	**2.50**
1874-1876	Bust of William Crawford.	**1.50**

Confederate States of America

Torn, frayed or excessively worn notes command little or no premium.

PAPER MONEY ISSUES

All notes were issued from Richmond, Virginia, except the few 1861 issues listed as from Montgomery, Alabama.

In recent years, facsimiles have been made of many Confederate notes. Many people mistake them for genuine pieces. They are usually on much heavier paper and are invariably in new condition. In many cases, the word, "Facsimile" may actually be found in quite small letters somewhere on the note.

Confederate notes will sometimes be found cut or slit in a regular pattern, or with holes punched through. These indicate cancellation by the Confederacy, and are worth less than uncancelled specimens.

For further general comment on Confederate currency, please see under "United States Paper Money" in the General Information following the Preface.

50 CENT NOTES

Year	*Portrait or Main Design*	*Used*
1863	Jefferson Davis. Blank Rev.	**1.25**
1864	Similar to above except for date.	**1.00**

1 DOLLAR NOTES

1862	Steamship with sails; female standing at left; Lucy Pickens at right. Blank Rev.	**3.00**
1862	Similar to above, but overprinted with a large green "1" and "ONE." Blank Rev.	**5.00**
1862	C. Clay. Blank Rev.	**4.00**
1863	Similar to above except for date.	**3.25**
1864	Similar to above except for date.	**1.00**

2 DOLLAR NOTES

1861	The "South" attacking the "North" with sword; J. P. Benjamin at left. Blank Rev.	**25.00**
1862	The "South" attacking the "North" with sword; J. P. Benjamin at left. Blank Rev.	**3.25**
1862	Similar to above but overprinted with a large green "2" and "TWO." Blank Rev.	**14.50**
1862	Ornamented "2" in center; J. P. Benjamin at right. Blank Rev.	**2.50**
1863	Similar to above except for date.	**2.50**
1864	Similar to above except for date.	**2.00**

5 DOLLAR NOTES

1861	Liberty seated with shield and eagle, a "5" in front; sailor at left. Blank Rev.	**200.00**
1861	"V" in upper left; "5" in upper right. Blue Rev.	**200.00**
1861	Five females seated; standing female at left; Washington at right. Blank Rev.	**22.50**
1861	Child at left; blacksmith at right. Blank Rev.	**27.50**
1861	C. Memminger; Minerva at right, "V" below. Blank rev.	**13.00**
1861	Similar to above except that "FIVE" is below Minerva. Blank Rev.	**5.00**

Year	Portrait or Main Design	Used
1861	Blacks loading cotton on ship at left; Indian girl at right. Blank Rev.	225.00
1861	Female seated on cotton bale; sailor at left. Blank Rev.	3.00
1861	Sailor and cotton bales; C. Memminger at left; two females at right. Blank Rev.	3.00
1862	State Capitol at Richmond, Va.; C. Memminger at right. Blue Rev.	2.00
1863	Similar to above except for date.	2.00
1864	Similar to above except for date.	1.50

10 DOLLAR NOTES

Year	Portrait or Main Design	Used
1861	Liberty seated with shield and eagle; female at left. Blank Rev.	3.00
1861	Indian family; female with trident at left; female with "X" at right. Blank Rev.	30.00
1861	Cotton wagon; male bust at left; harvester at right. Blank Rev.	35.00
1861	R. Hunter at left; a child at right. Blank Rev.	12.00
1861	Female with anchor; R. Hunter at left; C. Memminger at right. Blank Rev.	5.00
1861	Similar to above except that an "X" is overprinted in red at each side of the female. Blank Rev.	5.00
1861	Liberty with eagle and shield at upper left; small train at right. Blank Rev.	250.00
1861	Two females with urn at upper left; small train at right. Blank Rev.	2.00
1861	Black with cotton; landscape at right. Blank Rev.	6.00
1861	Military figures at dinner; R. Hunter at left; Minerva at right. Blank Rev.	3.00
1862	Female leaning on cotton bales, ships in rear; R. Hunter at right. Blank Rev.	3.00
1862	Female seated with wheat; R. Hunter at right. Blank Rev.	600.00
1862	State Capitol at Columbia, S. C.; R. Hunter at right. Blue Rev.	1.50
1863	Similar to above except for date.	1.50
1864	Horses pulling artillery pieces; R. Hunter at right. Blue Rev.	1.50

20 DOLLAR NOTES

Year	Portrait or Main Design	Used
1861	Full masted sailing ship. Blank Rev.	2.50
1861	Three females in center, Liberty standing at left. Blank Rev.	60.00
1861	Full masted sailing ship; sailor at left. Blank Rev.	2.00
1861	Female with globe; female at left; blacksmith at right. Blank Rev.	200.00
1861	Female between Cupid and beehive; Vice President Stephens at left; female with anchor at right. Blank Rev.	1.75
1861	Vice President Stephens. Blank Rev.	17.50
1862	Liberty seated with shield of the Confederacy; R. Hunter at right. Blank Rev.	400.00
1862	State Capitol at Nashville, Tenn.; Stephens at right. Blue Rev.	4.00
1863	Similar to above except for date.	1.50
1864	Similar to above except for date.	1.25

50 DOLLAR NOTES

Year	Portrait or Main Design	Used
1861	Three black farm workers. Blank Rev. Montgomery, Ala.	500.00
1861	Two females on cotton bale; Justice at left; Washington at right. Blank Rev.	60.00
1861	Washington in center; seated figure at left. Blank Rev.	8.00
1861	Female and money chests; two sailors at left. Blank Rev.	3.00

Year	Portrait or Main Design	Used
1861	Railroad train; female with anchor at left; female with scales at right. Blank Rev.	225.00
1861	Jefferson Davis. Blank Rev.	6.00
1862	Jefferson Davis. Green Rev.	5.00
1863	Similar to above except for date.	5.00
1864	Similar to above except for date and a Blue Rev.	2.00

100 DOLLAR NOTES

1861	Railroad train in center; Liberty at left. Blank Rev. Montgomery, Ala.	700.00
1861	Railroad train in center; Justice at left; Minerva at right. Blank Rev.	65.00
1861	Two females in cloud; Washington at left. Blank Rev.	50.00
1861	Blacks loading cotton wagon; sailor at left. Blank Rev.	3.00
1862	Railroad train; milkmaid at left. Blank Rev.	2.00
1862	Blacks in cotton field; J. C. Calhoun at left; Liberty at right. Blank Rev.	3.00
1862	Lucy Pickens; two soldiers at left; Randolph at right. Green Rev.	17.50
1863	Similar to above except for date.	5.50
1864	Similar to above except for date and a Blue Rev.	1.50

500 DOLLAR NOTES

1861	Train on bridge; cattle below. Blank Rev. Montgomery, Ala.	1,750.00
1864	Confederate flag over horseman at left; "Stonewall' Jackson at right. Blank Rev.	20.00

1,000 DOLLAR NOTE

1861	John C. Calhoun and Andrew Jackson. Blank Rev. Montgomery, Ala.	1,950.00

CONFEDERATE COIN ISSUES

No Confederate coin was ever struck for actual circulation. However, four genuine trial specimens of a half dollar were allegedly struck. The reverse die of this coin was used at a later date to manufacture restrikes and it is these restrikes which appear on the market. Genuine U.S. half dollars of 1861 were used for this purpose, the reverse being planed off and then struck with the Confederate die.

The so-called Confederate Cent of 1861 shows a Liberty Head on the Obv. and the value on the Rev. A few specimens were struck privately in Philadelphia at the instigation of the Confederacy, but no coins were ever delivered. Both restrikes and modern replicas exist of this coin.

CONFEDERATE SILVER HALF DOLLAR.	1861	Fine	**400.00**
CONFEDERATE COPPER CENT.	1861	Proof	**1,250.00**

THE COINAGE OF BRITISH NORTH AMERICA

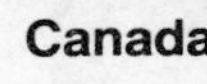

Canada

LARGE CENTS

Head of Queen Victoria

Date	*Amount Minted*	*Value*
1858	421,000	**15.00**
1859	9½ million	**.50**
1876-H	4 million	**.50**
1881-H	2 million	**.75**
1882-H	4 million	**.30**
1884	2½ million	**.30**
1886	1½ million	**.65**
1887	1½ million	**.65**
1888	4 million	**.30**
1890-H	1 million	**1.50**
1891 Large date	1½ million	**1.50**
1891 Small date	Part of above	**20.00**
1892	1¼ million	**.40**
1893	2 million	**.30**
1894	1 million	**1.00**
1895	1¼ million	**.60**
1896	2 million	**.40**
1897	1½ million	**.40**
1898-H	1 million	**1.25**
1899	2½ million	**.40**
1900	1 million	**1.50**
1900-H	2⅔ million	**.30**
1901	4 million	**.30**

Head of King Edward VII

Date	*Amount Minted*	*Value*
1902	3 million	**.25**
1903	4 million	**.25**
1904	2½ million	**.30**
1905	2 million	**.30**
1906	4 million	**.25**
1907	2½ million	**.25**
1907-H	800,000	**3.00**
1908	2⅓ million	**.25**
1909	4 million	**.20**
1910	5 million	**.20**

Head of King George V

Date	*Amount Minted*	*Value*
1911	4⅔ million	**.20**
1912	5 million	**.15**
1913	5¾ million	**.15**
1914	3½ million	**.25**
1915	4¾ million	**.25**
1916	11 million	**.15**
1917	12 million	**.15**
1918	13 million	**.15**
1919	11¼ million	**.15**
1920	7 million	**.15**

SMALL CENTS

Head of King George V

Date	*Amount Minted*	*Value*
1920	15½ million	**.04**
1921	7½ million	**.06**
1922	1¼ million	**3.00**
1923	1 million	**6.00**
1924	1½ million	**1.00**
1925	1 million	**3.50**
1926	2¼ million	**.50**
1927	3½ million	**.25**
1928	9 million	**.03**
1929	12¼ million	**.03**
1930	2½ million	**.40**
1931	3¾ million	**.20**
1932	21⅓ million	**.02**
1933	12 million	**.02**
1934	7 million	**.05**
1935	7½ million	**.05**
1936	8¾ million	**.05**

Head of King George VI

(The following valuations are for coins in brilliant, new condition, and showing no signs of wear. Used or circulated Cents from 1937 to date do not command a premium.)

		NEW			NEW
1937	10 million	.50	1946	56⅔ million	.10
1938	18⅓ million	.50	1947	31 million	.50
1939	21⅔ million	.50	1947 Maple leaf	43¾ million	.35
1940	85¾ million	.25	1948	24¾ million	.50
1941	56⅓ million	2.50	1949	33⅓ million	.25
1942	76 million	2.00	1950	60½ million	.25
1943	89 million	1.00	1951	80½ million	.10
1944	44¼ million	2.00	1952	67⅔ million	.10
1945	77½ million	.10			

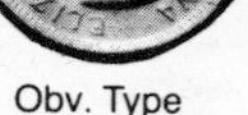
Obv. Type 1953-1964

Rev. Type 1937-

Obv. Type 1965-

Commemorative Rev. 1967

Head of Queen Elizabeth II

(The valuations are for coins in brilliant, new condition)

		NEW			NEW
1953	72¼ million	.20	1970	311¼ million	.01
1954	22 million	.50	1971	298¼ million	.01
1955	56⅔ million	.10	1972	451⅓ million	.01
1956	78⅔ million	.10	1973	457 million	.01
1957	100½ million	.10	1974	692 million	.01
1958	57¾ million	.10	1975	642⅓ million	.01
1959	83⅔ million	.05	1976	701 million	.01
1960	75¾ million	.05	1977	453 million	.01
1961	139½ million	.05	1978	911 million	.01
1962	227¼ million	.05	1979	754 million	.01
1963	279 million	.05	1980	911¾ million	.01
1964	484⅔ million	.05	1982	876 million	.01
1965	304½ million	.01	1983	975½ million	.01
1966	183⅔ million	.01	1984	838¼ million	.01
1967	345¼ million	.01	1985		.01
1968	329⅔ million	.01	1986		.01
1969	335¼ million	.01	1987		.01
			1988		.01

SILVER 5 CENTS

Head of Queen Victoria

(The following valuations are for coins in G-VG condition)

Date	*Amount Minted*	*Value*	*Date*	*Amount Minted*	*Value*
1858 Small date	1½ million	**2.50**	1887	500,000	**5.00**
1858 Large date	Part of above	**50.00**	1888	1 million	**1.10**
1870	2¾ million	**1.50**	1889	1¼ million	**6.00**
1871	1½ million	**1.50**	1890-H	1 million	**1.00**
1872-H	2 million	**1.00**	1891	1¾ million	**1.10**
1874-H	800,000	**1.75**	1892	860,000	**1.25**
1875-H	1 million	**40.00**	1893	1¾ million	**1.00**
1880-H	3 million	**.75**	1894	500,000	**2.75**
1881-H	1½ million	**1.00**	1896	1½ million	**1.00**
1882-H	1 million	**1.00**	1897	1⅓ million	**1.00**
1883-H	600,000	**1.50**	1898	580,717	**2.00**
1884	200,000	**37.50**	1899	3 million	**.75**
1885	1 million	**1.50**	1900	1¾ million	**.75**
1886	1¾ million	**1.10**	1901	2 million	**.75**

Head of King Edward VII

Date	Amount Minted	Value	Date	Amount Minted	Value
1902	2 million	**.50**	1906	3 million	**.50**
1902-H	2¼ million	**.50**	1907	5¼ million	**.45**
1903	1 million	**.70**	1908	1¼ million	**1.50**
1903-H	2⅔ million	**.50**	1909	1¾ million	**.75**
1904	2⅓ million	**.50**	1910	6 million	**.55**
1905	2⅔ million	**.50**			

Head of King George V

Date	*Amount Minted*	*Value*	*Date*	*Amount Minted*	*Value*
1911	3⅔ million	**.60**	1917	5⅔ million	**.35**
1912	5¾ million	**.35**	1918	5¾ million	**.35**
1913	5½ million	**.35**	1919	8 milion	**.35**
1914	4¼ million	**.35**	1920	10⅔ million	**.35**
1915	1¼ million	**1.50**	1921	2½ million	**800.00**
1916	2⅓ million	**.60**			

NICKEL 5 CENTS

Head of King George V

Date	Amount Minted	Value	Date	Amount Minted	Value
1922	4¾ million	**.06**	1930	3⅔ million	**.07**
1923	2½ million	**.07**	1931	5 million	**.06**
1924	3 million	**.06**	1932	3¼ million	**.07**
1925	200,050	**10.00**	1933	2½ million	**.07**
1926	933,577	**1.00**	1934	3¾ million	**.06**
1927	5¼ million	**.06**	1935	3¾ million	**.06**
1928	4½ million	**.06**	1936	4⅓ million	**.06**
1929	5½ million	**.06**			

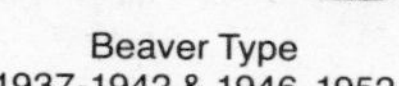

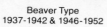

Beaver Type
1937-1942 & 1946-1952

V for Victory
1943-1945

Nickel
Bicentennial
1951

Head of King George VI

Beginning with the 1942 Tombac issue, the shape of the nickel is 12-sided, rather than round

Date	*Amount Minted*	*Value*	*Date*	*Amount Minted*	*Value*
1937	5 million	.05	1946	7 million	.05
1938	4 million	.05	1947	7⅔ million	.05
1939	5⅔ million	.05	1947 Maple Leaf	9½ million	.05
1940	14 million	.05	1948	1¾ million	.15
1941	8⅔ million	.05	1949	13 million	.05
1942-Nickel	6¾ million	.05	1950	12 million	.05
1942 Tombac	3⅓ million	.08	1951 Regular	4⅓ million	.05
1943	24¾ million	.05	1951 Commem.	9 million	.05
1944	11½ million	.05	1952	10¾ million	.05
1945	18¾ million	.05			

12-sided 1953-1962
Round 1963-1964

Mature Head Type
1965-

Commemorative
Rev. 1967

Head of Queen Elizabeth II

		NEW			NEW
1953	16⅔ million	.50	1971	27⅓ million	.05
1954	7 million	.75	1972	62½ million	.05
1955	5⅓ million	.50	1973	53½ million	.05
1956	9⅓ million	.25	1974	94¾ million	.05
1957	7⅓ million	.25	1975	138.8 million	.05
1958	7½ million	.25	1976	55 million	.05
1959	11½ million	.10	1977	89 million	.05
1960	37 million	.07	1978	137 million	.05
1961	47¾ million	.06	1979	186¼ million	.05
1962	46¼ million	.06	1980	134¾ million	.05
1963	44 million	.06	1981	99 million	.05
1964	78 million	.05	1982	105½ million	.05
1965	84¾ million	.05	1983	72½ million	.05
1966	27½ million	.05	1984	84 million	.05
1967	58¾ million	.05	1985		.05
1968	99¼ million	.05	1986		.05
1969	27¾ million	.05	1987		.05
1970	5¾ million	.05	1988		.05

10 CENTS

Head of Queen Victoria

Date	*Amount Minted*	*Value*
1858	1¼ million	**3.00**
1870	1⅔ million	**2.75**
1871	800,000	**3.00**
1871-H	1¾ million	**4.75**
1872-H	1 million	**20.00**
1874-H	600,000	**2.25**
1875-H	1 million	**60.00**
1880-H	1½ million	**2.25**
1881-H	950,000	**3.25**
1882-H	1 million	**1.75**
1883-H	300,000	**4.50**
1884	150,000	**70.00**
1885	400,000	**3.25**
1886	800,000	**3.00**
1887	350,000	**2.75**
1888	500,000	**2.75**
1889	600,000	**175.00**
1890-H	450,000	**2.75**
1891	800,000	**2.75**
1892	520,000	**2.25**
1893 Flat top 3	500,000	**2.25**
1893 Round top 3	Part of above	**175.00**
1894	500,000	**1.75**
1896	650,000	**1.25**
1898	720,000	**1.25**
1899	1¼ million	**.75**
1900	1 million	**.50**
1901	1¼ million	**.50**

Head of King Edward VII

Date	Amount Minted	Value	Date	Amount Minted	Value
1902	720,000	**.50**	1906	1⅔ million	**.50**
1902-H	1 million	**.50**	1907	2⅔ million	**.50**
1903	500,000	**.75**	1908	761,631	**.50**
1903-H	1⅓ million	**.50**	1909	1½ million	**.50**
1904	1 million	**.75**	1910	4⅔ million	**.50**
1905	1 million	**.65**			

Head of King George V

Date	Amount Minted	Value	Date	Amount Minted	Value
1911	2¾ million	**2.75**	1921	2½ million	**.30**
1912	3¼ million	**.30**	1928	2½ million	**.30**
1913 Small leaves	3½ million	**.30**	1929	3¼ million	**.30**
1913 Large leaves	Part of above	**20.00**	1930	1¾ million	**.30**
1914	2½ million	**.30**	1931	2 million	**.30**
1915	672,408	**.30**	1932	1¼ million	**.30**
1916	4¼ million	**.30**	1933	672,368	**.30**
1917	5 million	**.30**	1934	384,056	**.30**
1918	5 million	**.30**	1935	384,592	**.30**
1919	7¾ million	**.30**	1936	2¾ million	**.30**
1920	6¼ million	**.30**			

Head of King George VI

Date	Amount Minted	Value	Date	Amount Minted	Value
1937	2½ million	**.45**	1946	6⅓ million	**.25**
1938	4¼ million	**.25**	1947	4½ million	**.25**
1939	5½ million	**.25**	1947 Maple leaf	9⅔ million	**.25**
1940	16½ million	**.25**	1948	422,741	**1.25**
1941	8¾ million	**.25**	1949	11⅓ million	**.25**
1942	10¼ million	**.25**	1950	17¾ million	**.25**
1943	21¼ million	**.25**	1951	15 million	**.25**
1944	9⅓ million	**.25**	1952	10½ million	**.25**
1945	11 million	**.25**			

Obv. Type 1953-1964

Rev. Type 1937-

Obv. Type 1965-

Commemorative Rev. 1967

Head of Queen Elizabeth II

Date	*Amount Minted*	*Value*	*Date*	*Amount Minted*	*Value*
1953	18½ million	**.25**	1970	5¼ million	**.10**
1954	4½ million	**.25**	1971	41 million	**.10**
1955	12¼ million	**.25**	1972	60 million	**.10**
1956	16¾ million	**.25**	1973	167¾ million	**.10**
1957	15⅔ million	**.25**	1974	201½ million	**.10**
1958	11 million	**.25**	1975	207⅔ million	**.10**
1959	19⅔ million	**.25**	1976	95 million	**.10**
1960	45½ million	**.25**	1977	128½ million	**.10**
1961	26¾ million	**.25**	1978	170⅓ million	**.10**
1962	41¾ million	**.25**	1979	237 million	**.10**
1963	42 million	**.25**	1980	169¾ million	**.10**
1964	49½ million	**.25**	1981	124 million	**.10**
1965	57 million	**.25**	1982	94 million	**.10**
1966	34⅓ million	**.25**	1983	111 million	**.10**
1967	63 million	**.25**	1984	119 million	**.10**
1968 Silver	70½ million	**.20**	1985		**.10**
1968 Nickel	107 million	**.10**	1986		**.10**
1969	55¾ million	**.10**	1987		**.10**
			1988		**.10**

20 CENTS

Head of Queen Victoria

1858	750,000	**20.00**

25 CENTS

Head of Queen Victoria

Date	Amount Minted	Value	Date	Amount Minted	Value
1870	900,000	**3.75**	1887	100,000	**30.00**
1871	400,000	**4.50**	1888	400,000	**2.75**
1871-H	748,000	**4.50**	1889	66,340	**30.00**
1872-H	2¼ million	**3.25**	1890-H	200,000	**3.25**
1874-H	1⅔ million	**3.25**	1891	120,000	**7.00**
1875-H	1 million	**85.00**	1892	510,000	**2.75**
1880-H	400,000	**4.25**	1893	100,000	**7.00**
1881-H	820,000	**3.50**	1894	220,000	**2.75**
1882-H	600,000	**3.75**	1899	415,580	**2.50**
1883-H	960,000	**2.50**	1900	1⅓ million	**2.00**
1885	192,000	**30.00**	1901	640,000	**2.00**
1886	540,000	**2.75**			

Head of King Edward VII

Date	Amount Minted	Value	Date	Amount Minted	Value
1902	464,000	**1.10**	1906	1¼ million	**1.10**
1902-H	800,000	**1.10**	1907	2 million	**1.10**
1903	846,150	**1.10**	1908	466,625	**1.10**
1904	400,000	**1.10**	1909	1⅓ million	**1.10**
1905	800,000	**1.10**	1910	3½ million	**1.10**

Head of King George V

Date	Amount Minted	Value
1911	1⅔ million	**3.75**
1912	2½ million	**1.00**
1913	2¼ million	**1.00**
1914	1¼ million	**1.00**
1915	238,378	**2.00**
1916	1½ million	**1.00**
1917	3¼ million	**.75**
1918	4¼ million	**.75**
1919	5¾ million	**.75**
1920	2 million	**.75**
1921	575,268	**2.00**
1927	468,096	**7.00**
1928	2 million	**.75**
1929	2⅔ million	**.75**
1930	961,174	**1.00**
1931	537,815	**1.00**
1932	537,994	**1.00**
1933	421,282	**1.25**
1934	384,505	**1.25**
1935	537,997	**1.25**
1936	972,094	**.75**
1936 Dot below date	153,685	**7.00**

Head of King George VI

Date	Amount Minted	Value
1937	2⅔ million	**.65**
1938	3¼ million	**.65**
1939	3½ million	**.65**
1940	9½ million	**.65**
1941	6⅔ million	**.65**
1942	7 million	**.65**
1943	13½ million	**.65**
1944	7¼ million	**.65**
1945	5¼ million	**.65**
1946	2¼ million	**.65**
1947	1½ million	**.65**
1947 Maple leaf	4⅓ million	**.65**
1948	2½ million	**.65**
1949	8 million	**.65**
1950	9⅔ million	**.65**
1951	8¼ million	**.65**
1952	8¾ million	**.65**

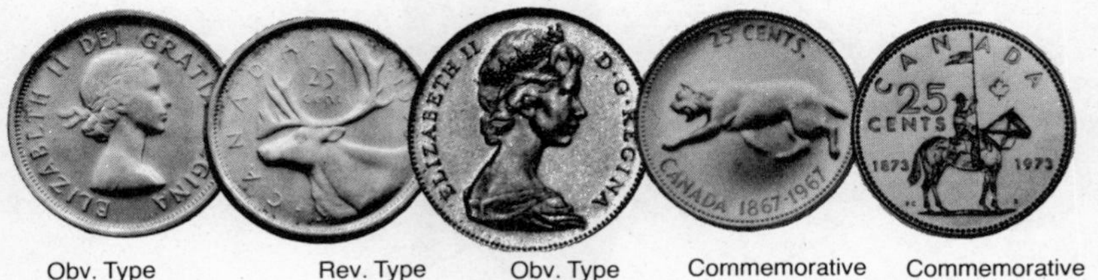

Obv. Type 1953-1964 — Rev. Type 1937- — Obv. Type 1965- — Commemorative Rev. 1967 — Commemorative Rev. 1973

Head of Queen Elizabeth II

Date	*Amount Minted*	*Value*
1953	11¼ million	**.65**
1954	2⅓ million	**.65**
1955	9½ million	**.65**
1956	11¼ million	**.65**
1957	12⅓ million	**.65**
1958	9¾ million	**.65**
1959	13½ million	**.65**
1960	22¾ million	**.65**
1961	18¼ million	**.65**
1962	29½ million	**.65**
1963	21¼ million	**.65**
1964	36½ million	**.65**
1965	44¾ million	**.65**
1966	25⅓ million	**.65**
1967	48¾ million	**.65**
1968 Silver	71½ million	**.50**
1968 Nickel	88⅔ million	**.25**
1969	133 million	**.25**
1970	10⅓ million	**.25**
1971	48 million	**.25**
1972	43¾ million	**.25**
1973	135 million	**.25**
1974	192⅓ million	**.25**
1975	141 million	**.25**
1976	86.8 million	**.25**
1977	99⅔ million	**.25**
1978	176½ million	**.25**
1979	131 million	**.25**
1980	76 million	**.25**
1981	131½ million	**.25**
1982	131 million	**.25**
1983	167 million	**.25**
1984	119¼ million	**.25**
1985		**.25**
1986		**.25**
1987		**.25**
1988		**.25**

50 CENTS

Head of Queen Victoria

Date	*Amount Minted*	*Value*	*Date*	*Amount Minted*	*Value*
1870	450,000	**15.00**	**1892**	**151,000**	**17.50**
1871	200,000	**20.00**	1894	29,036	**60.00**
1871-H	45,000	**30.00**	1898	100,000	**17.50**
1872-H	80,000	**12.50**	1899	50,000	**22.50**
1881-H	150,000	**12.50**	1900	118,000	**12.50**
1888	60,000	**30.00**	1901	80,000	**12.50**
1890-H	20,000	**200.00**			

Head of King Edward VII

1902	120,000	**2.25**	1907	300,000	**2.50**
1903-H	140,000	**3.00**	1908	121,260	**2.50**
1904	60,000	**25.00**	1909	198,648	**2.50**
1905	40,000	**25.00**	1910	640,141	**2.50**
1906	350,000	**2.50**			

The valuations listed in this book closely approximate how much established coin dealers will pay for any material needed in their stock.

Head of King George V

Date	Amount Minted	Value
1911	204,475	**2.50**
1912	283,248	**2.00**
1913	263,290	**2.00**
1914	157,537	**10.00**
1916	454,853	**2.00**
1917	739,715	**2.00**
1918	832,805	**2.00**
1919	1 million	**2.00**
1920	559,521	**2.00**
1921	176,793	**2,500.00**
1929	228,021	**2.00**
1931	57,581	**2.50**
1932	19,213	**20.00**
1934	38,435	**2.50**
1936	38,550	**2.50**

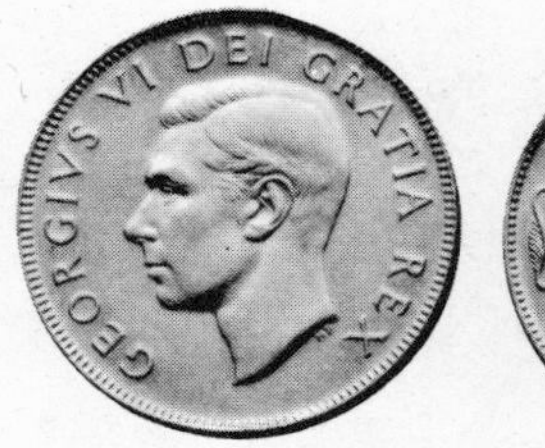

Head of King George VI

Date	Amount Minted	Value
1937	192,016	**2.00**
1938	192,018	**2.00**
1939	287,976	**2.00**
1940	2 million	**1.50**
1941	1⅔ million	**1.50**
1942	2 million	**1.50**
1943	3 million	**1.50**
1944	2½ million	**1.50**
1945	2 million	**1.50**
1946	950,235	**1.50**
1947	424,885	**2.00**
1947 Maple leaf, straight 7.	38,433	**7.00**
1947 Maple leaf, curved 7.	Part of above.	**400.00**
1948	37,784	**17.50**
1949	858,991	**2.00**
1950	2⅓ million	**2.00**
1951	2½ million	**1.50**
1952	2½ million	**1.50**

(The valuations in this book are based on the coins being in G-VG condition, unless otherwise noted.)

Obv. Type 1953-1964 | First Rev. Type 1953-1958 | Second Rev. Type 1959- | Commem. Rev. 1967 | Obv. Type 1965-

Head of Queen Elizabeth II

Head of Queen Elizabeth II

Date	*Amount Minted*	*Value*	*Date*	*Amount Minted*	*Value*
1953	1¾ million	**1.25**	1971	2¼ million	**.50**
1954	506,305	**1.25**	1972	2½ million	**.50**
1955	753,511	**1.25**	1973	2½ million	**.50**
1956	1⅓ million	**1.25**	1974	3½ million	**.50**
1957	2¼ million	**1.25**	1975	3¾ million	**.50**
1958	3 million	**1.25**	1976	3 million	**.50**
1959	3 million	**1.25**	1977	709,939	**1.00**
1960	3½ million	**1.25**	1978	3⅓ million	**.50**
1961	3½ million	**1.25**	1979	3½ million	**.50**
1962	5¼ million	**1.25**	1980	1½ million	**.50**
1963	8⅓ million	**1.25**	1981	2¾ million	**.50**
1964	9⅓ million	**1.25**	1982	2⅓ million	**.50**
1965	12⅔ million	**1.25**	1983	2¼ million	**.50**
1966	7⅔ million	**1.25**	1984	1¼ million	**.50**
1967	4¼ million	**1.25**	1985		**.50**
1968 Nickel, reduced size, 4 mil.		**.50**	1986		**.50**
1969	7⅓ million	**.50**	1987		**.50**
1970	2½ million	**.50**	1988		**.50**

SILVER DOLLARS

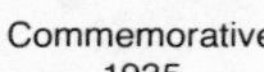
Commemorative
1935

Regular Issue
1936

Rev. Type
1935-1936

Head of King George V

		Used	*Unc*			*Used*	*Unc*
1935	428,120	**4.00**	**20.00**	1936	306,100	**4.00**	**20.00**

Obv. Type
1937-1952

Regular Rev.
1937-1952

Commemorative Rev.
1939

Commemorative Rev.
1949

Head of King George VI

Date	*Amount Minted*	*Used*	*Unc*
1937	241,002	**3.50**	**25.00**
1938	90,304	**5.00**	**50.00**
1939	1⅓ million	**3.50**	**12.00**
1945	38,391	**40.00**	**150.00**
1946	93,055	**7.50**	**70.00**
1947 Blunt 7	65,595	**20.00**	**80.00**
1947 Pointed 7	Part of above	**50.00**	**350.00**
1947 Maple leaf	21,135	**70.00**	**300.00**
1948	18,780	**250.00**	**700.00**
1949	672,298	**4.00**	**20.00**
1950	261,002	**4.00**	**15.00**
1951	420,620	**3.50**	**12.00**
1952	408,835	**3.50**	**12.00**

Obv. Type
1953-1964

Regular Rev. Type

Obv. Type
1965-

Commemorative Rev.
1958

Commemorative Rev.
1964

Commemorative Rev.
1967

Commemorative Rev.
1970

Commemorative Rev.
Nickel—1971

Commemorative Rev.
Silver—1971

Commemorative Rev.
Nickel—1973

Commemorative Rev.
Silver—1973

Commemorative Rev.
1974

Commemorative Rev.
Silver—1975

Commemorative Rev.
Silver—1976

Commemorative Rev.
Silver—1977

Note: From 1981 onwards, .500fine silver dollars exist in both proof-like (Unc) and, only as parts of sets, proof.

Head of Queen Elizabeth II

Date	Amount Minted	Used	Unc
1953	1 million	3.00	7.00
1954	242,815	4.00	9.00
1955	274,810	4.00	9.00
1956	209,092	4.50	9.00
1957	496,389	3.00	5.00
1958	3 million	3.00	9.00
1959	1½ million	3.00	5.00
1960	1½ million	3.00	5.00
1961	1¼ million	3.00	5.00
1962	1¾ million	3.00	5.00
1963	4¼ million	3.00	5.00
1964	7¼ million	3.00	5.00
1965	10¾ million	3.00	5.00
1966	10 million	3.00	5.00
1967	7 million	3.00	5.00
1968	Nickel, reduced size, 6 mil.		1.00
1969	4¾ million		1.00
1970	4¼ million		1.00
1971	Nickel 4¼ million		1.00
1971	Silver, proof-like, cased, 555,564		5.00
1972	Nickel 2⅔ million		1.00
1972	Silver, proof-like, cased, 350,019		5.00
1973	Nickel 3¼ million		1.00
1973	Silver, proof-like, cased, 709,670		5.00
1974	Nickel 2¾ million		1.00
1974	Silver, proof-like, cased, 977,644		5.00
1975	Nickel 3¼ million		1.00
1975	Silver, proof-like, cased 931,000		5.00
1976	Nickel 2½ million		1.00
1976	Silver, proof-like cased, 483,722		5.00
1977	Nickel 1⅓ million		1.00
1977	Silver, proof-like, cased, 744,848		5.00
1978	Nickel 3 million		1.00
1978	Silver, proof-like, cased, 709,602		5.00
1979	Nickel 2½ million		1.00
1979	Silver, proof-like, cased, 826,695		5.00
1980	Nickel 3⅓ million		1.00
1980	Silver, proof-like, cased, 539,617		10.00
1981	Nickel 2¾ million		1.00
1981	Silver, proof-like, cased, 699,494		10.00
1982	Nickel 1 million		1.00
1982	Nickel, Constitution 9¾ million		1.00
1982	Silver, proof-like, cased, 903,888		7.00
1983	Nickel 2¼ million		1.00
1983	Silver, proof-like, cased, 159,400		5.00
1984	Nickel, 1¼ million		1.00
1984	Nickel, Cartier 7 million		1.00
1984	Silver, proof-like, cased, 133,610		4.00
1985	Nickel		1.00
1985	Silver, proof-like, cased,		4.00
1986	Nickel		1.00
1986	Silver, proof-like, cased,		7.00
1987	Nickel		1.00
1987	Silver, proof-like, cased,		6.00

Olympic Commemorative Coins

The same obverse, the head of Queen Elizabeth II, appears on all of the coins. The valuations are for coins in brilliant, new condition.

SERIES I, 1973

Denomination	*Date*	*Reverse Design*	
5 Dollars	1973	Map of North America	5.50
5 Dollars	1973	Kingston Skyline	5.50
10 Dollars	1973	Map of the World	11.00
10 Dollars	1973	Montreal Skyline	11.00
4-piece Uncirculated Set, cased			32.50
4-piece Proof Set, cased			40.00

SERIES II, 1974

Denomination	*Date*	*Reverse Design*	*Value*
5 Dollars	1974	Athlete with Olympic Torch	**5.50**
5 Dollars	1974	The Laurel Wreath	**5.50**
10 Dollars	1974	The Greek God, Zeus	**11.00**
10 Dollars	1974	The Temple of Zeus	**11.00**
4-piece Uncirculated Set, cased			**32.50**
4-piece Proof Set, cased			**40.00**

SERIES III, 1974

5 Dollars	1974	Canoeing	**5.50**
5 Dollars	1974	Rowing	**5.50**
10 Dollars	1974	Cyclists	**11.00**
10 Dollars	1974	Lacrosse	**11.00**
4-piece Uncirculated Set, cased			**32.50**
4-piece Proof Set, cased			**40.00**

SERIES IV, 1975

5 Dollars	1975	Marathon	**5.50**
5 Dollars	1975	Javelin	**5.50**
10 Dollars	1975	Hurdles	**11.00**
10 Dollars	1975	Shotput	**11.00**
4-piece Uncirculated Set, cased			**32.50**
4 piece Proof Set, cased			**40.00**

SERIES V, 1975

5 Dollars	1975	Swimming	**5.50**
5 Dollars	1975	Diving	**5.50**
10 Dollars	1975	Sailing	**11.00**
10 Dollars	1975	Kayak	**11.00**
4-piece Uncirculated Set, cased			**32.50**
4-piece Proof Set, cased			**40.00**

SERIES VI, 1976

5 Dollars	1976	Fencing	**5.50**
5 Dollars	1976	Boxing	**5.50**
10 Dollars	1976	Soccer	**11.00**
10 Dollars	1976	Field hockey	**11.00**
4-piece Uncirculated Set, cased			**32.50**
4-piece Proof Set, cased			**40.00**

SERIES VII, 1976

5 Dollars	1976	Olympic Village	**5.50**
5 Dollars	1976	Olympic Flame	**5.50**
10 Dollars	1976	Olympic Stadium	**11.00**
10 Dollars	1976	Olympic Velodrome	**11.00**
4-piece Uncirculated Set, cased			**32.50**
4-piece Proof Set, cased			**40.00**

CALGARY WINTER OLYMPICS, 1988

20 Dollars	1985	Downhill Skier	**17.50**
20 Dollars	1985	Speed Skater	**17.50**
20 Dollars	1986	Biathlon	**17.50**
20 Dollars	1986	Hockey	**17.50**
20 Dollars	1986	Cross Country Skier	**17.50**
20 Dollars	1986	Free Style Skier	**17.50**

GOLD COINS

Canadian Types

Head of King George V

5 DOLLARS

Date	*Amount Minted*	*Value*
1912	165,680	**150.00**
1913	98,832	**150.00**
1914	31,122	**450.00**

10 DOLLARS

1912	74,759	**400.00**
1913	149,232	**400.00**
1914	140,068	**450.00**

Head of Queen Elizabeth II

5 DOLLARS

1982	246,000	**30.00**
1983	198,000	**30.00**
1984	262,000	**30.00**
1985		**30.00**
1986		**30.00**
1987		**30.00**
1988		**30.00**

10 DOLLARS

1982	184,000	**85.00**
1983	192,000	**85.00**
1984	313,000	**85.00**
1985		**85.00**
1986		**85.00**
1987		**85.00**
1988		**85.00**

20 DOLLARS

1967	337,512 proofs	**150.00**

50 DOLLARS

Maple Leaf Gold Bullion Coins

Date	*Amount Minted*	*Value*	*Date*	*Amount Minted*	*Value*
1979	1 million	**375.00**	1984	1,002,000	**375.00**
1980	1¼ million	**375.00**	1985		**375.00**
1981	863,000	**375.00**	1986		**375.00**
1982	883,000	**375.00**	1987		**375.00**
1983	776,000	**375.00**	1988		**375.00**

100 DOLLARS

1976 27 mm. Olympics (.585) 572,387 proofs	**80.00**	1982 Constitution 200,000 proofs	**150.00**
1976 25 mm. Olympics 335,779 proofs	**125.00**	1983 St. John's 82,000 proofs	**200.00**
1977 Jubilee 180,396 proofs	**250.00**	1984 Cartier 67,000 proofs	**170.00**
1978 Geese 200,000 proofs	**150.00**	1985 National Parks 200,000 proofs	**200.00**
1979 Children 250,000 proofs	**150.00**	1986 Peace proofs	**180.00**
1980 Eskimo 300,000 proofs	**150.00**	1987 Calgary Olympics Proofs	**175.00**
1981 National Anthem 102,000 proofs	**150.00**	1988 Whales	**150.00**

English Type Sovereigns or Pounds

Normal type Gold 1 Pound pieces of English design, struck at the Ottawa Mint and with the "C" mint mark on the ground under the horse. The coins from 1908 through 1910 are with the head of Edward VII and those from 1911 through 1919 are with the head of George V.

1 Pound 1908-C	636	**750.00**	1 Pound 1914-C	14,891	**150.00**
1 Pound 1909-C	16,273	**150.00**	1 Pound 1916-C	6,111	**Rare**
1 Pound 1910-C	28,012	**125.00**	1 Pound 1917-C	58,845	**85.00**
1 Pound 1911-C	256,946	**80.00**	1 Pound 1918-C	106,516	**85.00**
1 Pound 1913-C	3,715	**250.00**	1 Pound 1919-C	135,889	**85.00**

Newfoundland
(complete from 1865 to 1947)

LARGE CENTS

Head of Queen Victoria

Date	*Amount Minted*	*Value*	*Date*	*Amount Minted*	*Value*
1865	240,000	**.30**	1885	40,000	**4.50**
1872-H	200,000	**.30**	1888	50,000	**3.75**
1873	200,025	**.30**	1890	200,000	**.30**
1876-H	200,000	**.30**	1894	200,000	**.30**
1880	400,000	**.30**	1896	200,000	**.30**

Head of King Edward VII

1904-H	100,000	**.75**	1909	200,000	**.30**
1907	200,000	**.30**			

Head of King George V

Date	Amount Minted	Value
1913	400,000	.15
1917-C	702,350	.15
1919-C	300,000	.15
1920-C	302,184	.15
1929	300,000	.15
1936	300,000	.15

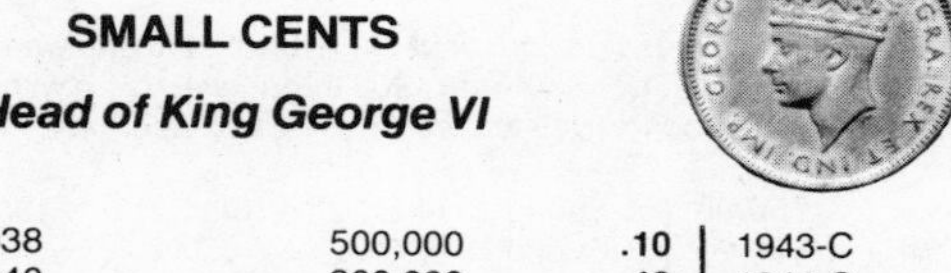

SMALL CENTS

Head of King George VI

1938	500,000	.10
1940	300,000	.40
1941-C	827,662	.10
1942	2 million	.10
1943-C	1¼ million	.10
1944-C	1⅓ million	.10
1947-C	313,772	.10

SILVER 5 CENTS

Head of Queen Victoria

1865	80,000	**6.00**
1870	40,000	**6.50**
1872-H	40,000	**6.00**
1873	44,260	**6.50**
1873-H	Part of above	**100.00**
1876-H	20,000	**10.00**
1880	40,000	**6.50**
1881	40,000	**3.75**
1882-H	60,000	**3.00**
1885	16,000	**20.00**
1888	40,000	**3.75**
1890	160,000	**2.50**
1894	160,000	**2.50**
1896	400,000	**1.50**

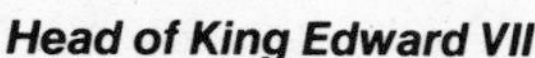

Head of King Edward VII

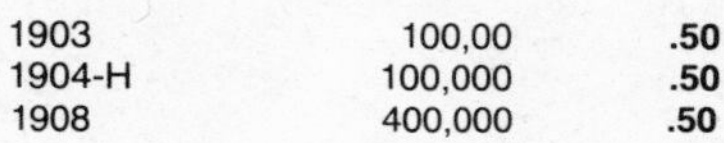

1903	100,00	**.50**
1904-H	100,000	**.50**
1908	400,000	**.50**

Head of King George V

Date	Amount Minted	Value
1912	300,000	**.50**
1917-C	300,319	**.50**
1919-C	100,844	**.50**
1929	300,000	**.50**

Head of King George VI

Date	Amount Minted	Value
1936	100,000	**.30**
1940-C	200,000	**.30**
1941-C	612,641	**.30**
1942-C	298,348	**.50**
1943-C	351,666	**.30**
1944-C	286,504	**.30**
1945-C	203,828	**.30**
1946-C	2,041	**90.00**
1947-C	38,400	**.50**

10 CENTS

Head of Queen Victoria

Date	Amount Minted	Value
1865	80,000	**5.00**
1870	30,000	**75.00**
1872-H	40,000	**5.00**
1873	23,614	**5.00**
1876-H	10,000	**7.00**
1880	10,000	**7.00**
1882-H	20,000	**5.00**
1885	8,000	**25.00**
1888	30,000	**5.00**
1890	100,000	**2.00**
1894	100,000	**2.00**
1896	230,000	**2.00**

Head of King Edward VII

Date	Amount Minted	Value
1903	100,000	**.60**
1904-H	100,000	**.60**

Head of King George V

Date	Amount Minted	Value
1912	150,000	**.60**
1917-C	250,805	**.60**
1919-C	54,342	**.60**

Head of King George VI

Date	Amount Minted	Value	Date	Amount Minted	Value
1938	100,000	.45	1944-C	151,471	.45
1940	100,000	.45	1945-C	175,833	.45
1941-C	483,630	.45	1946-C	38,400	**50.00**
1942-C	292,736	.45	1947-C	61,988	**1.00**
1943-C	104,706	.45			

20 CENTS

Head of Queen Victoria

1865	100,000	**3.00**	1885	40,000	**1.25**
1870	50,000	**4.00**	1888	75,000	**1.25**
1872-H	90,000	**3.00**	1890	100,000	**1.25**
1873	45,797	**3.00**	1894	100,000	**1.25**
1876-H	50,000	**3.00**	1896	125,000	**1.25**
1880	30,000	**1.50**	1899	125,000	**1.25**
1881	60,000	**1.25**	1900	125,000	**1.25**
1882-H	100,000	**1.25**			

Head of King Edward VII

1904-H	75,000	**1.50**

Head of King George V

Date	*Amount Minted*	*Value*	*Date*	*Amount Minted*	*Value*
1912	350,000	**1.25**			

25 CENTS

Head of King George V

Date	*Amount Minted*	*Value*	*Date*	*Amount Minted*	*Value*
1917-C	464,779	**1.50**	1919-C	163,939	**1.50**

50 CENTS

Head of Queen Victoria

Date	*Amount Minted*	*Value*	*Date*	*Amount Minted*	*Value*
1870	50,000	**3.00**	1885	40,000	**3.00**
1872-H	48,000	**3.00**	1888	20,000	**3.00**
1873	37,675	**3.00**	1894	40,000	**3.00**
1874	80,000	**3.00**	1896	60,000	**3.00**
1876-H	28,000	**4.00**	1898	76,607	**3.00**
1880	24,000	**4.00**	1899	150,000	**3.00**
1882-H	100,000	**3.00**			

Head of King Edward VII

Date	*Amount Minted*	*Value*	*Date*	*Amount Minted*	*Value*
1904-H	140,000	**3.00**	1908	160,000	**3.00**
1907	100,000	**3.00**	1909	200,000	**3.00**

Head of King George V

1911	200,000	**2.00**	1918-C	294,824	**2.00**
1917-C	375,560	**2.00**	1919-C	306,267	**2.00**

GOLD COINS

2 DOLLARS

Head of Queen Victoria

1865	10,000	**140.00**	1881	10,000	**100.00**
1870	10,000	**140.00**	1882-H	25,000	**100.00**
1872	6,050	**170.00**	1885	10,000	**100.00**
1880	2,500	**700.00**	1888	25,000	**100.00**

New Brunswick

(All coins are with the head of Queen Victoria)

Coin	*Date*	*Amount Minted*	*Value*
Half Cent	1861	222,800	**15.00**
Large Cent	1861	1 million	**.25**
Large Cent	1864	1 million	**.25**

Silver 5 Cents	1862	100,000	**10.00**
Silver 5 Cents	1864	100,000	**10.00**
10 Cents	1862	150,000	**7.50**
10 Cents	1864	100,000	**7.50**
20 Cents	1862	150,000	**4.00**
20 Cents	1864	150,000	**4.00**

Nova Scotia

(All coins are with the head of Queen Victoria)

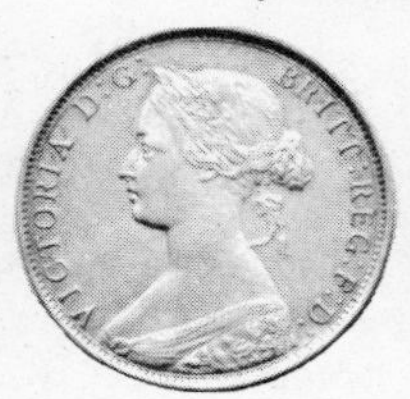

Half Cent	1861	460,000	**1.25**
Half Cent	1864	400,000	**1.25**
Large Cent	1861	800,000	**.25**
Large Cent	1862	100,000	**3.50**
Large Cent	1864	800,000	**.25**

Prince Edward Island

(Head of Queen Victoria)

Coin	*Date*	*Amount Minted*	*Value*
Large Cent	1871	1 million	**.25**

British Columbia

Very rare gold coins that were not placed in circulation

Coin	Date	Amount Minted	Value
10 Dollars	1862		—
20 Dollars	1862		—

(The valuations in this book are based on the coins being in G-VG condition, unless otherwise noted.)